My YORKSHIRE
GREAT *and* SMALL

YORKSHIRE VET
PETER WRIGHT

*To my dear daughter Emily,
son Andrew, and lovely grandson Archie,
in the hope that he will appreciate
Yorkshire as much as his Grandad.*

PETER WRIGHT

First published by Mirror Books in 2019

Mirror Books is part of Reach plc
10 Lower Thames Street,
London EC3R 6EN

www.mirrorbooks.co.uk

ISBN 978-1-912624-64-5

Typeset by Danny Lyle
DanJLyle@gmail.com

1 3 5 7 9 10 8 6 4 2

Every effort has been made to fulfil requirements with regard to
reproducing copyright material. The author and publisher will be
glad to rectify any omissions at the earliest opportunity.

Cover images: Paul Gay/iStockphoto
All other images courtesy of: Peter Wright, iStockphoto, yorkshire.com, Mirrorpix, Alex Telfer, Alamy.

CONTENTS

With Georgey Spanswick of BBC Radio York, at The Great Yorkshire Show

The Great Yorkshire Show

"Come on Peter! Strip off your jacket and tie!"

It's rare for a woman to ask me to remove my clothes nowadays, especially when my wife Lin is watching. But an order is an order; I felt I had no choice but to do as I was told. The formidable, and rather scary, lady barking at me made me feel like a naughty schoolboy. Lin had a huge grin on her face and was thoroughly enjoying my discomfort, as I meekly stood there in my shirt and trousers, wondering what on earth I had got myself into and what would happen next. But it was too late to back out now. I would just have to accept my fate. When I'd stripped down to my shirtsleeves, the well-known chef and TV personality Rosemary Shrager handed me a full-length cream apron. I took a deep breath and told myself the ordeal, in front of a live audience of at least 250 people, would soon be over.

I've got nothing against Rosemary, of course – quite the opposite. I'd met her for the first time at an awards ceremony for community heroes a few weeks before. We'd got on well and I'd told her how impressed I was by her culinary skills and her no-nonsense character. I'd also told her that I'd like to learn how to cook. I can't really conjure up anything in the kitchen, unless you count egg and chips, and beans on toast. Lin is the chef in our house. If we've had an argument and I'm in the doghouse and expected to cook my own tea, I have trouble even working the hob. Luckily, Lin usually takes one look at my helplessness and takes pity on me. Rosemary knew I was out of my comfort zone in the kitchen, and when she invited me to cook with her at the Great Yorkshire Show in Harrogate, she'd initially thought I would turn her down.

The three-day show, which takes place in July, has been one of the biggest fixtures of the British agricultural calendar for more than 150 years. This year it was being filmed for a two-part TV special called *Today at the Great Yorkshire Show*, made by Daisybeck Studios, creators of *The Yorkshire Vet*. Rosemary and I were among several TV people invited to appear in the programme. Paul Stead, Daisybeck's boss, had persuaded me to do a few new things on camera, including some cooking. Apparently, he thought *Yorkshire Vet* fans would enjoy seeing me grapple with kitchen implements and a rack of lamb, instead of surgical instruments and a pain-racked lamb, if you will excuse my attempt at humour.

So there I was, in the show's food hall and specially built "cookery theatre". I had a small microphone clipped to my lapel and a three-person film crew hovering directly in front of me, which irritated a woman who'd been delighted to bag a seat in the first row, but could now see very little of the demonstration, as her view was blocked by two cameras and an enormous fluffy mic.

"You know, of course, where a lamb's ribs are, but can you butcher this?" Rosemary asked me in her crisp southern accent, beaming as she pointed at two large pieces of raw and bony meat lying on the worktop in front of us. We were, she said, going to make lamb, gnocchi and crispy kale. It would apparently be drizzled with a "jus", which we all know is just a fancy name for gravy.

It sounded so simple and, indeed, it was for Rosemary. Hardly pausing for breath as she kept up a seemingly effortless running commentary, she showed me how to use a knife to cut the rack of lamb "against the bone". She then showed me which bits of fat to scrape off. It took her several minutes to explain as she demonstrated with the first piece of lamb. I watched intently. I didn't want to show myself up and, more importantly, I didn't want to give Lin any more reason to laugh. She was already cackling like a mad hen – I hadn't seen her have this much fun in years. Soon Rosemary was searing the first bit of lamb and making little balls of herby, cheesy gnocchi while I began cutting up "my" piece of meat.

"You're doing well, Peter," she boomed. I wiped my brow. "You're awfully quiet," she added a little while later.

"I'm a little lamb, I'm trying to do as I'm told," I muttered.

"That would be a first!" Lin shouted out from the crowd.

Enemy fire on two fronts, I thought.

"No, no, no!" said Rosemary. "Not like that!"

Eventually, after adding a breadcrumb, cheese and anchovy topping to her piece of lamb, Rosemary put it in the oven while I continued to chop and scrape.

"Do you operate on animals, Peter?" the chef asked brightly, adding, "You're still not doing this right."

I pointed out that I had never done it before. "But I have got into a rib cage inside an animal," I said.

In the end, the meat preparation took me so long that I didn't have a chance to do anything else, other than stir a bit of butter into the redcurrant sauce, or jus, or gravy. I told Rosemary I couldn't multi-task, but she certainly can, and it was fascinating to work alongside her.

As she cooked, she told the crowd that her great-grandfather had lived in a North Yorkshire village after working as an engineer in China. He'd even brought flamingos over. She high-fived me as we heard her pontificate on everything from her love of learning and Yorkshire produce to left- and right-handed lobsters and her worries about the meat industry. "We need to eat less meat for the climate," she said, suddenly serious. I didn't like to point out that she was cooking lamb. "But our farmers are amazing and need our support," she added.

I fully agreed. "British beef, lamb and pork are the best in the world," I said.

Soon it was time to taste our – or rather Rosemary's – meaty creation, all beautifully presented on a plate with the jus expertly drizzled over the top. It's hard to describe how delicious it was. The flavours were truly gorgeous. The kale was perfectly salty and crunchy, while the lamb simply melted in my mouth. I stood there gnawing on a succulent bone, meat juice dripping from my chin as the audience looked on, some of them drooling in envy. "You are a genius, Rosemary," I said.

A few minutes later Lin and I were sitting at the back of a little buggy being driven to our next appointment by Joe, a Leeds university student on a work placement. I'm sure he would have liked to get us there quicker, but it wasn't to be. For one thing, he had to drive me to the toilet first. Secondly, there were a lot of people wandering around – we didn't want to kill anyone by going too fast – and then Lin dropped the little pot of jus/gravy out of the doggy bag Rosemary had given us containing the meal "I" had just cooked. Joe had to stop the buggy almost before we had set off so we could pick it up from the grass. Luckily, it hadn't burst open. Phew, I thought: that would have been a sorry end to the sauce.

I'd been rushing from pillar to post all morning. I wasn't complaining, though, because there was so much to see and there was still time for the odd bit of fun. One of the film crew gave us all a laugh by managing to catch an escaped sheep, straddling the animal as she scurried past. It was actually my second day at the show – the day before, I'd been flouncing around on a catwalk. I'm obviously far more used to dealing with actual cats but, as it was my second time strutting my stuff, I like to think I've learned to walk the walk. I was told by one woman to "imagine you are a peacock". I thoroughly enjoyed twirling and flashing open my tweed jacket with what I'm convinced was utter panache. I'd also been filmed for *Today at the Great Yorkshire Show*. Lin and I had even tasted several Yorkshire gins for the programme. Although she rarely drinks alcohol, my wife somehow managed to attach herself to a rather unfair nickname: Gin Lin. She didn't seem to mind.

We stayed in a nearby hotel after our gin-tasting session, as we had to be up early for the second day of the show, which every year attracts thousands of humans and animals. They come together to compete, socialise and celebrate this great county of ours. Before my date with Rosemary, I had a few hours of activities lined up, including two interviews with BBC Radio York's Georgey Spanswick, who was broadcasting live from the event. I've known Georgey for a while now; I've even treated her dog. Our first chat, at about 7.45am, took place just after her listeners had heard from the National Vegetable Society's Geoff Wilson, who lives in North Yorkshire. My mouth was watering as I listened to him describe his prize-winning vegetables, including cauliflowers, peas and onions. Geoff said that a lot more young people were needed in the Society and I would have liked to talk to him about how that might be achieved. He's right, more youngsters do need to take an interest in agriculture if the sector is to flourish.

Sadly I had no time to chat to Geoff about ravishing rhubarb and the future of farming. For, not far from where some beautifully turned out and beautifully groomed horses were being paraded in a big ring while classical music played, I was on air discussing Yorkshire, my career, and the need for many more new vets. It was so early that the first visitors had only just started arriving. A man in a kilt was playing the bagpipes at one of the showground's ten gates. Every year, about 130,000 people attend the event, as well as 8,500 animals, from bees and sheep to horses and cattle. They're the real stars.

The first show was held in 1838, with the first attendance figures taken in 1842: a very specific 6,044 visitors were recorded. In the early years, the show took place in no fewer than 30 different towns before a decision was made to build a permanent showground near Harrogate. With the growing popularity of *The Yorkshire Vet*, I've become increasingly involved in the Great Yorkshire Show. I've often been filmed discussing the animals being shown and the hopes and expectations of their owners, some of them my friends.

As I stood waiting to do another interview, a BBC employee told me she was disappointed there were no pigs in this year's show, as she loved them. It certainly was a shame. But we both knew there had been a last-minute suspected case of swine dysentery in a pig at a show elsewhere and so, wisely, no pigs had been allowed to take part in Harrogate. At that point, a smartly dressed man approached me and introduced himself. He was a farmer with land in Scotland and Devon. He was also one of the show's equine judges. We chatted about his Texel sheep possibly having hay fever; they were sneezing and had runny noses, he said. I'd never come across hay fever in sheep before, and wondered if it was a low-grade viral pneumonia.

Just then, Amanda Owen popped up. She's written a series of books about farming and looking after sheep, and is known as the *Yorkshire Shepherdess*. Tall and glamorous, she looked pretty relaxed considering she is a hill farmer – at one of the highest farms in England – and has nine children. It was probably a nice break to visit the show, I thought. It was good to see her again and, although I can't recall why, we had a quick chat about how you never have binoculars when you need them. She told me she often travels to distant objects that she thinks are sheep, only to discover they are nothing more than rocks. She said binoculars would save her a lot of time. I told her I still didn't have a pair. I've been trying to buy some for ten years, but can't decide which ones would be both decent quality and good value for money.

There seemed to be plenty of *Yorkshire Vet* fans at the show who didn't need binoculars. I was stopped everywhere by people who just wanted a chat. It was heart-warming.

"'Ow are ya, Peter?" one middle-aged man called out.

"Not so bad," I said, as Joe slowly, oh so slowly, drove Lin and me in the buggy towards our next destination. "I'm just saving my shoe leather," I joked, cringing slightly at being ferried around. Who did I think I was?

"You're just like Moses, parting the Red Sea," said a woman as we inched our way through the crowds, which moved apart to let us through.

"I'm like a lamb to the slaughter," I grinned.

I was often asked to pose for photographs – and was delighted to do so. One snap in particular stood out. Nine-year-old Summer Ali, from Bradford, was at the event for the very first time with her dad, Paul, and his partner, Sadie. Summer asked to have her picture taken with me. I always enjoy meeting *Yorkshire Vet* fans, but it's extra special to talk to children who enjoy it. She liked the programme so much, she'd even written a brilliant poem for me the night before. She read it out to me; it was the highlight of my day. It's called *Peter Wright*, and goes like this:

Peter Wright is a good vet, alright!
He has helped dogs and maybe the odd frog,
He saved hissing cats with the behaviour of wild bats,
He saved a rabbit with a very bad habit of licking its thumb
then wiping its bum,
He's very keen to cheer up Mr and Mrs Green,
If your sheep is sick or your pony has flu
Peter Wright is the one for you.

At one point, I was lucky enough to take in the view from above the showground in a traffic helicopter. What a scene lay before me: a thriving temporary town in the North Yorkshire countryside, surrounded by horseboxes, cars and campervans.

Back on earth again, I got to look around a few of the multitude of activities going on. In the Woodland Information Centre, where the Forestry Commission pointed out it was celebrating its 100th birthday, a man was sat carving a face from a piece of wood, while nearby, visitors read about the need to plant more trees. In an art show a few metres away, the face of a smiling pig looked down from the wall near a painting of a loaf of bread and a small stucco statue of a sheep. In the Women's Institute room, a former teacher wove wonderful willow baskets while visitors tucked into cream teas.

"Think global, act local" said a poster near a display of items made from single-use plastics, which were being judged for a competition. The winning entry was a plastic, and very lovely, purple hydrangea. Elsewhere, people were looking at scores of handsome and puffed-up pigeons, while not far away other visitors jostled for free crackers, chutney and crumbly cubes of Wensleydale cheese. Small children played, laughed and screamed in a sandpit under a massive photograph of the beach at Bridlington. There were food stalls and ice creams galore. I caught a mere glimpse of all manner of gleaming farm machinery. But there were so many other things on display, too, that I didn't manage to see – the show's 250 acres seemed almost impossible to cover.

I couldn't do everything, but I was determined to see as many animals as possible. I deliberately made a beeline for the donkeys, as I became The Donkey Sanctuary charity's first ever ambassador this year, on its 50th anniversary. I know just how important it is to look after these wonderful creatures. Too often they are treated shoddily, in Britain and further afield.

Of course, most of the donkeys taking part in the Great Yorkshire Show's competitions were in no need of the charity, although it does rescue some that go on to successfully compete. That's an amazing feat, given where they come from. I made my way into an area where several donkeys stood waiting to be judged. They all looked to be in perfect health. A trio of Miniature Mediterraneans caught my eye, so I chatted to their owners, John and Lorraine Rae from Northumberland. Both were dressed in smart show suits and pristine hats, and Lorraine was holding the reins of a donkey called Frontier Legends Diplomat, or Diplomat for short, who was six years old and just 29 inches high. Born in Texas, he seemed a docile but engaging animal; he was friendly and cuddly. He'd won many awards at various shows and it sounded like he lived a fine life, running around a paddock or grazing for hours at a time. He was the father of an eight-week-old foal called Rhinestone Cowboy; another of his offspring was due to be born soon. I crouched down to pat Diplomat's two friends, Daisy Bouquet and Wind in the Willow, while owner John gave them bits of liquorice allsorts. "They like ginger biscuits and bananas too," he said.

Sadly, I couldn't hang around, but it was good to hear later on that little Diplomat had come first in his donkey class. Next, I went to see some cattle. Growing up on a farm, I've been around cows in one way or another since I was a child, but I don't work with them nearly as much these days. Very few of my clients are farmers now, as small farms are slowly but surely dying away. Thankfully, the Great Yorkshire Show is still somewhere to see all kinds of breeds of cattle in all their glory, up close and personal. I popped into one of the sheds and saw several large red and white Longhorn cattle. Their long, curved horns can make them look aggressive, but they are usually friendly enough. These ones were relaxed, chewing their cud. Watching the animals lying there, doing what they do best, made me feel all was well in the world, as it always does. "They're so iconic," I said to their owner, a farmer from Northumberland.

I sat down on a bale of hay as we briefly discussed the pioneering 18th-century livestock breeder Robert Bakewell, the first to carry out systematic selective breeding. He only allowed very deliberate and specific mating. It sounds normal enough now, but it was revolutionary back then. Many of Bakewell's methods are still used today, and it was he who came up with today's Longhorns. Their big horns look very impressive, but they were actually bred to produce as much meat as possible, which was needed to feed people who were moving in to the towns and cities of the Industrial Revolution. It's a reminder that cattle are not just there to look at.

I was also particularly keen to see some Barnsley farming friends, the Nicholsons. They were showing Fern, their placid, shaggy red-haired Highland cow, and her mischievous calf, Ted, who likes to run off and cause chaos. A few months previously I'd been to a cattle auction in Scotland with Roger, who's in his 70s, to buy Fern. It had been a good trip, with two tight-fisted old Yorkshiremen trying to get a bargain from a Scot. But the sale eventually happened and we had come away with a beautiful animal. Roger, who owns Cannon Hall Farm, which is both a working farm and tourist attraction, had competed in many agricultural shows before, as had his late father Charlie. But this was the first time for Roger's two sons, David and Robert. They'd worked hard for weeks to prepare Fern and Ted for the prestigious Yorkshire event, and it was brilliant to see David overcome his nerves and proudly parade the two animals. It was the icing on the cake to see Fern win first prize in the senior heifer section. David's face was a picture as he was handed a red rosette and realised his hard work for the family had paid off. "It's like the Oscars for farmers," he said. I was just glad he didn't give an Oscar-style speech.

As the sun shone down I couldn't help but reflect on how lucky I was. I've been a vet now for the best part of four decades, learning from two of the best, Alf Wight and Donald Sinclair. Alf is better known as the author James Herriot; Donald was Siegfried Farnon in his books and the subsequent TV series and films. Alf managed to capture the life of a country vet perfectly. Although the job has changed a fair bit since Alf and Donald's day, it's still wonderful. I love making poorly animals well again, and my work also brings me into contact with wonderful people like the Nicholsons.

Above all, I can never forget that I live in what I think is Britain's finest county: Yorkshire. The Great Yorkshire Show is a reminder of all that is good about this wonderful land of ours: its hills, its moors, its towns, its people – its animals. Yorkshire has everything – and a lot more besides.

&

Peter at Steve Green's 90th birthday party... and the infamous cakes!

CHAPTER 1

A Birthday Bash

As the pulsating beat boomed from an old stereo that most of us would have thrown away years ago, it crossed my mind that rave music might not be the most appropriate choice for this particular event. But the thought slid away as quickly as it had popped up when I glanced at the old man whose birthday we were here to celebrate. If he wasn't bothered – and his smiling face looked the opposite of bothered – then who was I to find fault? Steve Green, a Yorkshire farmer I'd first met more than four decades earlier when I was a shy trainee vet with Alf Wight and Donald Sinclair, was turning 90. He seemed to be enjoying his milestone, one of the rare occasions he's been the centre of attention. But he wasn't taking selfies, or posting social media updates, or getting ready for a fancy dinner at a posh restaurant. He was merely living his life as he always had: discreetly and quietly. Just getting on with things, enjoying himself where possible, but not expecting much. And rarely, if ever, complaining. To me, Steve is a throwback to a bygone age.

A small barn on Steve's farm had been decorated to celebrate his birthday. Several "90" banners had been strung around, and a large table off to one side was overflowing with pork pies, rolls, crisps and biscuits. There were two big birthday cakes, one made by Steve's daughter, Sarah, the other created by a Wakefield cake maker. On the latter there were two model cows, two donkeys, a dog and a tractor – all edible. Both cakes took pride of place on a table at the back of the barn. A small ceramic model of the birthday boy's favourite tractor – a thoughtful birthday gift that even showed the real number plate – was sandwiched between them.

Steve and his wife Jeanie sat on chairs behind the cakes, amiably surveying the scene like medieval aristocrats holding forth at a banquet. Friends and relatives, from elderly ex-farmers to small children, milled around. Many tried to keep out of shot of the *Yorkshire Vet* film crew by escaping outside. Unfortunately Lin and I didn't have long at the party; we were booked on a train from Thirsk that afternoon to London for a charity event, before flying to Scotland for more filming. But I wouldn't have wanted to miss Steve's birthday bash. I wanted to pay my respects to a man who, although almost 30 years older than me, still gets up early every day to feed his dozen or so calves and his two donkeys, Sybil and Mabel. The donkeys were a present from my *Yorkshire Vet* colleague Julian to mark the Greens' 40th wedding anniversary, when they had renewed their marriage vows.

Steve's been a pensioner for a long time, but old age hasn't stopped him driving a tractor on the family's 35-acre farm. In fact, he has three of them, including his favourite, a much-repaired Ferguson. Jeanie calls it the Silver Dream Machine. "It's 68, the same age as me," she said recently. My birthday gift to Steve was a trip to see some more Ferguson tractors, which I hoped he'd enjoy. He's not bothered about material things so I thought it best to give him an experience. Tractors are part of his DNA. We have that in common: I've always loved them too.

Hard work is also ingrained in his character. Even on his birthday he'd only stayed in bed for an extra ten minutes, and had made sure he did some of his chores before opening his cards. That didn't surprise me. Steve has worked hard all his life. He was born on a farm about three miles from Whitby and was milking by hand from the age of eight. He had to leave school at 13 to help his father, who'd been injured in an accident.

"I thought it were grand to leave school. If I'd known, I would have wanted to stay there longer," said Steve, showing he'd gained some wisdom in his nine decades.

When he was a young man, farms were mostly smaller than they are now, and had fewer machines. They needed a lot more labourers to do the work, which was much harder physically than it is now. Steve is shrewd enough to know the olden days weren't always as golden as people remember them.

In 1944, aged 15, he moved further inland with his parents to a farm on the outskirts of Thirsk, and there they built up a herd of dairy cows. Steve has lived in the same house ever since, and must now be one of the oldest farmers in the country. After his father died in the 1960s, Steve and his mother kept the farm going, employing several workers to help them. In 1978, a couple of years after his mum's death, Steve and Jeanie got married and she began to learn about farming. "I learned to drive a tractor straight away," she said. She didn't have far to move, which suited her just fine: she's lived her whole life in the area. Jeanie was born in an army hut in a field next to Steve's farm. The land there had been used to house an army camp. Her father had joined the army and they were billeted there in temporary housing when she came along. Later, her family moved to a house just down the road.

Over the decades, the home shared by Steve and Jeanie Green has acquired a host of other characters. First and foremost is the Greens' daughter, but there's also an assortment of much-loved cows, dogs, cats and donkeys. During his long life, Steve has barely left Yorkshire, let alone been on an aeroplane. He and Jeanie only went to London for the first time recently, visiting a "donkey garden" exhibit at the Chelsea Flower Show. Steve wore shoes but wished he'd taken his wellies, as his feet were aching. He once told me he'd been to Derbyshire when he was about 19 "to get three cows. And I went to Penrith for a horse." Jean isn't at all bothered about travelling either. "If the good Lord wanted me to fly he'd have given me wings," she sometimes says.

"I've had good health. I've been lucky. I'm well looked after," said Steve, chatting to friends gathered in the cluttered living room of the three-bedroomed farmhouse, before everyone headed to the party in the barn. Birthday paraphernalia, including an ornament that had been made to look like the family's current dog, Reuben, surrounded him. It was a gift from his daughter, Sarah. There was also an assortment of other knick-knacks, artwork and photographs, most of them relating to animals. I was particularly taken by a framed sketch of Steve and Jeanie, showing them from behind. Hand-in-hand, they were wearing their everyday work clothes. A speech bubble had Jeanie saying to her husband: "Mind you don't fall in the shit!" She always looks out for him.

Back in the real world, Jeanie continued to look out for her husband, busying herself folding up newly washed clothes, including two pairs of Steve's long-johns, then beavering away in the tiny, busy kitchen, preparing yet more food. Then she popped out to feed a couple of two-month-old calves – Cinnamon and Nutmeg – with powdered milk made up in buckets, overseen by a pink flamingo balloon floating around in an empty byre.

Steve was having an easyish day, but he only really started to slow down on the advice of doctors in 2015. It was then that the Greens finally, reluctantly, stopped milking their cows (and stopped drinking unpasteurised milk), tearfully deciding to sell their small dairy herd. It was a period of time totally suited to the much-overused phrase "the end of an era". Now the couple rear a handful of calves, all of them named, just as the Greens' dairy herd always was. They take in calves when they're about two weeks old and look after them for a year or so. The different personalities of the individual animals are always noticed and appreciated.

"And just look at their gorgeous eyelashes," said Jeanie. As a calf called Hannah sucked Jeanie's finger, with Charlotte, Macaroni and Cheese looking on, she added, "They'll all be sold as sucklers, not for meat. I wouldn't want them to be slaughtered." These are cows used only for breeding. Jeanie's reluctance to send an animal to slaughter is a natural response from a woman who broke down and cried not long ago when a kitten she'd rescued had to be put to sleep because it had an incurable virus. As Jeanie said: "I'm a sucker for a furry face."

Raising a glass to Steve was the least I could do for a hardworking, kind old man who sometimes sits on a tractor writing short stories about animals. He's also known for putting pen to paper while his wife does the grocery shopping in Thirsk. He lives so simply, in a way my old bosses Alf and Donald would have been familiar with through their many trips to farms in the 1930s, 40s and 50s. I'm lucky to have experienced some of it first-hand myself. My own childhood was a medley of fun outside, running around and building dens on the farm my father and grandfather worked on in Thirkleby, a village not far from Thirsk. I also enjoyed another activity not experienced by many children today – fishing. A lot of them don't have the opportunity as they live in towns and cities, or they're too distracted by the online world. In contrast, my younger brother David and I had oodles of spare time, with no phones, PS4s or Xboxes to distract us. And we lived in stunning countryside with opportunities galore to explore and let our imaginations run riot.

One of our favourite days out was the annual fishing trip we took with our father and his friend Eric Marshall. We'd go, just for the day, to a stocked lake in the Moors, close to a grand estate named Arden Hall and the village of Hawnby. Only one day each year, but what a memorable one it always turned out to be. It was only about ten miles from home, but it felt like a grand adventure. Mary Queen of Scots is said to have slept at Arden Hall en route to her execution, but we kids were more excited to see Eric, who would arrive on his motorbike, than to tread in Mary's last few footsteps. Eric is still a dear family friend, who lights up our lives as well as his village. And I mean that quite literally: he puts up thousands of Christmas lights in his front garden every December.

David and I would be beside ourselves thinking about catching trout with Dad and Eric. If truth were told, we rarely caught much, but it was so exciting to get up early in the morning with the pigeons cooing. Soon we'd be rowing out to a peaceful spot with our picnic of home-baked bread, cakes and scones. Nowadays I rarely go fishing, as I don't have the time. It's a luxury that will have to wait until my retirement.

Talking of luxuries, when I pass the two-metre tall Grandfather clock standing in my hall at home, I'm reminded of yet another childhood haunt. This solid physical echo of my youth, which Lin and I bought in an auction years ago (it irked me that it turned out to be the most expensive item, but she had her heart set on it) apparently belonged to a girls' boarding school called Skellfield. The school was near the village of Topcliffe in the Vale of York, with the Moors to the east and the Dales to the west. I lived in the village from the age of 13 until I left for university, so Skellfield, a 73-roomed Georgian mansion, was a significant backdrop in the landscape of my teenage years. I remember occasionally messing around with my mates in this empty stately home after the school closed its doors for the last time in 1970.

The mansion is not far from the banks of the River Swale, where a few of us once built a rickety raft of oil drums and wooden planks. The building was owned for a few years in the 1840s and 50s – when it was extended, improved and partied in – by Yorkshire railway magnate George Hudson. Skellfield School itself had originally been founded in Ripon back in 1877, but moved to the magnificent Topcliffe building in the 1920s. Pupils had to abandon it during the Second World War, when it was used as RAF accommodation for Canadian troops based at Skipton-on-Swale. They apparently called it "Skeleton House" because of all the dead mice and rats. After Skellfield finally shut up shop, the building was turned into apartments for elderly people, no doubt charming and high-ceilinged ones. Then it opened as Queen Mary's School in 1985, which still turns out well-to-do young ladies today.

Back in the early 1970s, my friend's parents were caretakers at the then empty mansion. They lived in a cottage next door. The couple didn't seem to mind four of us (their two sons and my brother and me) entering this glorious old house for a nose around. I don't remember who thought of it, but we took up the sport of racing armchairs with castors on the polished oak floors. They didn't half go. Some of us would "drive" chairs and others would push, at what seemed like improbably high speeds. I doubt pupils at Queen Mary's have such adventures today – which is, I suppose, fair enough, given the expense of maintaining a big listed building. Queen Mary's school says pupils are encouraged "to take risks in a controlled environment and a lot of that is to do with adventure – so the girls swim, canoe and kayak in the river, camp out on the river banks, use our climbing wall and scaffolding poles, learn bush craft, build dens, climb trees – you get the picture". It does sound fun. But isn't it a shame that children nowadays have so much less freedom than my friends and I had? We roamed around freely in an uncontrolled environment and loved our lives in the countryside.

A fast and furious chair stampede in George Hudson's old mansion was not the only highlight of my youth. I also remember having fun in fields around Topcliffe for hours, playing cricket or kicking a football around. I didn't know then that the village had been mentioned in the Domesday Book. Nor did I know that on the land next door to where I batted and bowled, scored and missed goals, had stood Maiden Bower Castle, built by the famous Percy family, later of Alnwick Castle in Northumberland. An angry mob was said to have stormed the site in 1489 to murder Henry Percy, Fourth Earl of Northumberland, in protest at increased taxes. Some said the killing was actually in Thirsk, but I wasn't at all bothered about an ancient "wheredunnit" when I was young. In the 1970s I just knew much of my huge playground belonged to dairy farmer Wilf Barningham.

Wilf worked from morning 'til night, often still out with his 60 or so cows at 11 pm. He rarely went anywhere. He certainly never went on holiday – just like the Greens, and the handful of other old farmers I know. Wilf's whole life revolved around the farm and his precious cows, whose milk he would personally deliver round Topcliffe. When my family first moved there, it was still unpasteurised – superb and creamy raw milk that my brother and I drank in bucketloads. Just as I only drink regular pasteurised milk these days, there are many other things from the past that seem strange but endearing now. Alf once wrote, as James Herriot, about catching sight of four middle-aged siblings sitting in a row, jammed tightly on a wooden bench in their farmhouse kitchen. "They were not asleep, not talking or reading or listening to the radio – in fact they didn't have one – they were just sitting." It was a typical evening. The four had worked hard. They'd eaten. And would sit, it seemed, until bedtime.

Wilf is still with us, and I'm pretty sure that he has a television and radio. He certainly loves chitchat. During his milk round, my late father, an expert natterer, would regularly hold him up as they caught up on the gossip. Wilf still chews the fat with me when I pass by. His grandson has a few cows in the same place these days and his daughter does a milk round, although the Barninghams' cows don't produce the milk for it these days; they buy it in.

Alf Wight with his Jack Russell terrier, Hector, in the vet's office at 23 Kirkgate, Thirsk talking to a client.

CHAPTER 2

The Old Ways

I feel privileged to have known, and still know, the strong community spirit in rural Yorkshire. Thirlby is a tiny village about four miles east of Thirsk, where Alf lived for many years until his death. Donald was close by too, in his magnificent home, Southwoods Hall. Lin and I built a house in Thirlby in the 1990s and raised our children there. It's an awe-inspiring location on the edge of the Moors and a perfect antidote to a vet's rollercoaster day, dealing with the joy of life and the despair of death.

Being immersed in nature truly is a balm for the soul. Alf referred to Thirlby in his writing, although he didn't call it by its real name, he renamed it 'Hannerly'. When he went with his wife Joan to view a property there in the 1970s, they immediately snapped it up, confirming the deal through a handshake with the owner. Later, he said he wouldn't have swapped it for Buckingham Palace; it's not hard to understand why. He wrote that "the air had a gentle warmth, rich with the scent of May blossom and the medley of wild flowers that speckled the grass. In a little wood to our right, a scented lake of bluebells flooded the shady reaches of the trees. As we sat there three squirrels hopped one after another from a tall sycamore." His wife said it was a slice of heaven.

Lin and I thought so too, and our neighbours turned out to be as life-affirming as the landscape. We've enjoyed many social events with them. One particular night of the year, the night before Bonfire Night, known in Yorkshire as Mischief Night, was an evening that brought out the true spirit of the place, in keeping with the Yorkshire humour I'd grown up with.

Mischief Night is a kind of informal holiday when children and teenagers engage in pranks and minor vandalism, though nothing too extreme. I seem to remember it wasn't so much the kids, more often Thirlby men in their 30s, 40s and 50s causing good-natured mayhem – the inimitable Hunter family among them. Expert woodcarvers by day (Alf gave us one of their handmade tables as a wedding present), they were expert jokers by night. Mischief Night is not as popular now, but 25 years ago a resident might notice their garden gate had gone, to find it later up a tree. A few people got a bit irate, but mostly they joined in the fun.

But it didn't have to be Mischief Night for the jokers to be out and about. Once when I'd been to the pub and had one too many, I didn't make it home for the delicious dinner Lin had prepared. In the pub I'd told my mates, "It will be beans on toast now. I'll be in trouble." The next morning I found a cold and congealed plate of beans on toast outside our front door. I still don't know who left it there.

Another time a large group of us had been to a wedding in the village and returned home more than a little worse for wear. Lin and I were shattered as well as drunk, so we went straight to bed. Hearing a commotion in the back garden a few minutes later, we got up and peered out of our bedroom window, which looked out over the lawn. There we could see the silhouette of two grown men taking it in turns to erratically pedal a rickshaw around. It had been used by the bride and groom that day, and still had cans and ribbons trailing in its wake. When a can got caught in a wheel and the rickshaw could no longer move, Lin and I went down to find them trying to hide from us behind a bush. We had a few more cans with them in the moonlight before they staggered off down the road and we went back to bed, still giggling like children. The little vehicle was still in our garden in the morning. Its drunken occupants emerged from their homes hours later, hungover and with little recollection of cycling around and squashing our beautiful flowers.

Probably the saddest part about getting older is the growing number of people who are no longer with us, many of them lovely and quirky characters. And I don't just mean family, friends and colleagues. I'm also talking about those you meet for an hour here and there, or even just for a few minutes. A lot of individuals populate your life and have an impact, big or small. Jim Wight, Alf's son who was also a vet and is now retired, was expecting to see many of his old clients on *The Yorkshire Vet*. "Some I do but a lot I don't, and that's depressing," he said. "I'm so old now, many of my customers have gone."

Of course, Alf's favourite characters were often immortalised through his writing, and had a positive impact on millions. One big favourite with readers was a young vet with a walrus moustache, called Brian Nettleton (Calum Buchanan in the books). I was lucky enough to meet him when he visited Alf in the 1980s, many years after they'd worked together. Brian made a strong impression on me, partly because he'd moved overseas to the wilds of Nova Scotia and then Papua New Guinea; at that time, I'd been hardly anywhere. And I was amazed he had six children, as large families were not nearly as common as they had been.

Mostly, though, Brian was memorable because his reputation went before him. Meeting him was like meeting an old and very popular friend, one fondly remembered by farmers and other locals as "t' vet wi't badger". That was because, long before I worked at 23 Kirkgate with Alf and Donald, Brian used to drive out to see clients with his pet badgers in the car. They'd cause havoc, scratching and chewing up the seats. (Perhaps Brian didn't mind because the car belonged to his bosses, but they became increasingly exasperated by the damage his animals caused.) He'd often walk around with a badger called Marilyn draped around his neck. He was a great hit with most animals and had other unusual pets, even an owl and a monkey, keeping them all in his flat above the practice. Donald, predictably, worked himself into a frenzy about this ever-growing menagerie, although Brian's wife Martha soon got used to it. Many Yorkshire folk, me included, were saddened to hear of his death in a car crash abroad not long after I met him. I can't imagine we'll see his like again.

Other characters also affected me, and the way I view the world. When I was very young I used to go to a barber's shop in Thirsk, just off the market place. There, an old man called Ozzy Downes was the first man to snip my locks (my mother had done it until then). He did his utmost to keep me calm and amused. "Snip snip snow, snip snip snow, three little goblins all in a row," he'd chant over and over while he worked. Then he charged my mother sixpence and gave me half of it, thruppence, "for being good". He can't have earned much, always putting kindness before profit. And I knew many other people like him who didn't have much, but shared it nonetheless.

Ozzy and many other shopkeepers and businesses from my childhood have gone, but thankfully not all. H Lee and Sons, a butcher's set up by Thomas Lee in 1747 – yes, 1747 – is still around.

I used to enjoy seeing one of his 20th century descendants, Harry Lee, a grin on his face and banter up his sleeve, at Thirsk Auction Mart. There he'd choose the animals that would end up on his customers' plates. He was proud to be the only butcher's in the town to still have its own abattoir. After Harry died in 2014 the abbatoir disappeared to make way for houses.

Like most of my colleagues when our veterinary practice was still at Kirkgate, I regularly drank in Thirsk, often after work. I don't drink alcohol much now; I'd rather have a cup of tea. But I can find it rather emotional to visit the town's pubs, to be honest, and the Golden Fleece in particular. There are so many memories associated with the place, most of them good, but a little difficult to look back on now I'm in my 60s.

Alf, who was 40 years older than me, had been going to the Fleece for decades before I started accompanying him for the occasional pint in the 1980s after I qualified as a vet. He, headmaster Stephen King, and businessman Harry Whitton were regulars there. In my mind's eye I can easily imagine the men, three pillars of the community, sitting around a small round table on a Saturday evening. There'd have been a domino group playing nearby and the trio would have been quaffing their pints, perhaps a whisky or two, and discussing everything from the latest football scores to their favourite classical music. A stream of locals would have interrupted them throughout the evening to talk to them about work-related issues. That's always the way when you live, work and socialise in the same place.

Of course, nostalgia can be fun if you can move past any melancholy that accompanies the memories. Jim and I had a fantastic little trip not long ago, driving around country roads in the Moors and Dales for a TV special about the Herriot years. We knew some of the routes well, travelling on them often in the 1980s and 90s when a lot more of our clients were farmers. These days I deal with pets most of the time and they are usually brought in to the practice.

For our journey into the past, Jim and I hired an old-fashioned car, an Austin 7 like the one his father drove in the 1940s, and drove it, slowly, to some of his favourite parts of rural Yorkshire. Alf was a young father and pretty hard up at the start of his veterinary career. It would be many years before he wrote the Herriot books that made him a wealthy and famous man. But he often said his happiest days had been when his children Jim and Rosie were little. He'd drive out to remote farms with them laughing and singing in the back seat, and felt happiness touch him on the shoulder. Jim told me his father did the first eleven years of his professional life on call every night. Asked why, Alf had answered: "I was glad to be alive."

Driving the old car and talking about Alf and the olden days made Jim and me a little downcast. But we cheered up when we pulled up at Skeldale. Although I still work there, Jim retired years ago. But he'd agreed to visit to help me recreate our old boss Donald's favourite veterinary stunt (one mentioned in the Herriot books) for the TV special. Upstairs in the staffroom, in an old cabinet that used to sit in our Kirkgate practice, are several items from bygone eras. Relics probably suited to a museum, but ones I can't bring myself to part with, like the old chloroform muzzle we used on horses when we needed to knock them out for an operation. But Jim and I weren't there for the muzzle. We wanted to get our hands on the cabinet's iodine crystals.

Eighty or so years ago, if a farm horse had pus in its foot, Donald might drain the foul-smelling fluid and tip crystals into

With Jeanie Green at Stephen's 90th birthday party. We chatted about milking the cows the old-fashioned way, as the Greens always did until the animals were sold when Steve was 86.

the wound, telling the farmer he was disinfecting it. Then he'd add some turpentine and stand back, savouring the moment when the chemical reaction would cause plumes of purple smoke to suddenly erupt. Alf, with tongue firmly in cheek, used to describe this as the art of veterinary science.

The farmer would invariably be impressed at the sight, even though the beautifully coloured vapour was just for show; this was the tail end of the "quack" years, and many locals then had little education or scientific knowledge. They looked up to those who at least seemed as if they did. Of course, Donald was a qualified and experienced vet, but he also had a sense of humour and was sometimes a bit of a showman. When he and Alf and other vets began saving a lot more animals with new and improved medicines and techniques, based on real science, they were, for a while, truly revered. Alf said he was lucky to experience this. "They were golden times, when vets were like magicians with needles," he'd say.

Now here were Jim and I, two grey-haired men surrounded by boring office furniture, no infected horse or farmyard in sight. But we dutifully got into the spirit of the thing and added some turps to a few crystals. We held our breath and suddenly, there it was – a cloud of purple smoke. "We're still alive, Pete," Jim grinned. "But what would health and safety think?" I laughed.

I don't want to give the impression the olden days were always good and modern times are always bad. Life was not perfect in the so-called Herriot years. Many more people died a lot earlier, for starters; Steve Green for example, had siblings who died young. And food was sometimes scarce. Steve told me he had to eat a lot of really fatty bacon (more fat than bacon) whether he liked it or not.

"I had to like it," he said. Fortunately, there's been a lot of progress in many walks of life. Steve and Jeanie get to watch reality shows about American police on TV, for one.

But some progress isn't progress at all, and intensive farming and mass production is a case in point. To give you an example: previously, testing for tuberculosis on small farms kept our practice at Kirkgate going for years. It was such an important task that Alf even did some testing during his honeymoon in 1941. Now big veterinary practices have to submit a tender to get that kind of work, which has to be done on a large scale. At Skeldale we don't even test our own farming clients' livestock, even though it would be better for disease prevention if we did; vets always understand the health and personalities of individual creatures better if they see them regularly. They know exactly what's normal for them.

Alf recognised the value of moving with the times, often employing new graduates who could give him the very latest information, passing on what they'd learned at university. But he'd have hated supermarkets selling such cheap milk that small dairy farmers can't earn a living. That's a way of life he wouldn't have condoned. The Greens stopped producing milk to actually sell years ago, as it wasn't profitable. Jeanie's blunt about the way so much of the farming world has gone. "Before, the cow would know you were there, that you loved her and thought the world of her. Now it's all mass production and they need lots of injections. Ridiculous. Let's go back to little farms. When folks were happier with other people." The Greens' dairy herd was small and didn't need vaccinations. They had tests, for the likes of TB and brucellosis, but never had an outbreak.

When Lin and I said our goodbyes and left Steve Green's birthday party, I thought how it was a little ironic that if the couple hadn't become regulars on *The Yorkshire Vet*, popular with millions of TV viewers, it would have been easy to think their old-fashioned way of life was already extinct. It's not – not yet, anyway. But visiting their home is a bit like travelling back in time. Their unkempt farmhouse, lush green grass, braying donkeys and birdsong are a blast from the past. But the image of their home fades as soon as my foot touches the accelerator as I drive away, particularly as there's a modern housing estate 100 metres from the Greens' farm. It makes me feel gloomy. I know people need somewhere to live, but it seems out of place.

Lin and I hit the main road and the Saturday traffic as we headed to the station to catch our London train. The Greens' way of life is fast disappearing, that much is clear. But – and I'm glad there is a but – *The Yorkshire Vet* has encouraged and reinforced interest in our precious animals and an old-fashioned way of life. And that's a good thing. For what are any of us without our roots and the land and people that feed us?

CHAPTER 3

Food, Glorious Food

I can scarcely believe I've reached an age where the question of what to do when I retire keeps cropping up. What I do know, beyond a shadow of a doubt, is that I'd like to continue living in my current home, surrounded by all the wildlife and unspoilt views of those green Yorkshire fields. Moving to a town, even to my beloved Thirsk, and being hemmed in by shops, cafés, cars and people, would probably finish me off. We all need clean air, peace and quiet, and easy access to the countryside. I know I'm lucky; I count my blessings from the moment I wake up and look out of the window to that golden snatch of time at dusk when I see owls swooping by.

As to what I will do when I no longer have to go to work each day, I'm less sure. I certainly want to spend more time with my family and keep my hand in with the veterinary world (so to speak). I'd also like to find the time to go fishing and do some walking. And I'm always eager to tend my vegetable plot. I just wish more potatoes, onions and cabbages made it to my plate, rather than being nibbled by pesky rabbits, slugs and pigeons. To say nothing of the caterpillars and everyone else who enjoys my gardening efforts. Maybe they can let me know how it all tastes.

Talking about homegrown food brings to mind a friend of mine, Philip Shaw. Seventeen years older than me (although he doesn't look it) he's the right age to give me a bit of advice about retiring, especially as he's done it twice. He has 20 acres of land and is one of many Yorkshire farmers producing delicious food. His blissful little farm is just a few miles from my home and was once part of the Thirkleby Hall estate, where my great-grandfather Robert was a stonemason. Philip, a grandfather of five, grew up in the West Yorkshire countryside in the 1940s, near the cattle farm where his father worked, but for much of his own career he lived outside God's own country, in Shropshire. He was an engineer and retired early, at the age of just 50. But he quickly grew bored painting the house and tending the garden, so went back to work for nine years, travelling to the United States more than 40 times.

Eventually, Philip retired again, in the late 1980s. He loves cricket, and could have enjoyed his retirement following England on winter tours to exotic locations in the Caribbean and Sri Lanka, but did nothing of the sort. Instead, he and his wife Janet, a Yorkshirewoman who grew up on a dairy farm near Wetherby, bought six acres of Shropshire land and a few cows and sheep to, as Philip says, "cut the grass". While he studied at agricultural college as a mature student to learn all he could about lambing, ewe grading and calf rearing, Janet continued running her busy grocery store. When she sold it in 1989, the couple decided to move back to their roots in Yorkshire. That's when they bought the land they now live on, moving into its 18th-century former coaching inn made of Whitby stone. Philip's aim was to create a farm "like the ones around when I was a lad. Something simple with some livestock, but not masses of them. This place fulfils that." He tends to break even, he's told me, but he isn't in it for the money. "I love what I'm doing. Living here is all we hoped for. Life is simple, with purpose and nature." It's a way of life I wholeheartedly endorse: it's farming that is good for nature, good for the animals and produces wonderful products for us, the consumers.

Philip rears about a dozen Aberdeen Angus calves each year, buying them when they are about a week old from his farming nephew and selling them on when they are about 16 months, for breeding or to be fattened up for the butcher's knife. He also tends about 25 ewes and the 40 or so lambs they have between them each year. The meat they produce has an excellent reputation, often receiving top prices. On top of all that, he also has bees that make around 30 pounds of gorgeously sweet honey each year, as well as a well-maintained garden. There he grows plump and juicy gooseberries, thick, strong rhubarb, and pretty and nutritious lettuce. Finally, there are tasty fresh eggs from his three huge hens.

Whenever I drive through Philip's gates I feel a weight lifting from my shoulders. He's a man at one with the land and his animals, and it feels good to be there. He has found the perfect balance in his life. He mostly just farms, spending little time on other pursuits; he might go to market in Thirsk or York, or to watch a cricket match, but doesn't do much else. "I've already done all the travelling I want to do," he often says. Tall, upright and bursting with energy, he admits to arthritic hands and has had a knee replacement. Despite that, he and Janet, who's a year younger than him (another one who's drunk deeply at the fountain of youth), still enjoy walking a few miles a week.

Philip tends to his calves most days, feeding them with powdered milk when they're too young to graze. In the barn during winter or outside when the weather's better, he watches them closely for any sign of ill health or injury. I often see him patting and stroking them. "They come up to me and want a rub," he says. He knows all of them, and they know him.

It's the same with the sheep. They come running when he calls and he is not only interested in the mating, lambing, feeding and worming. Philip is fascinated by their personalities. "Some are nervous; some are super intelligent. There was one who could open any gate. She'd stand and watch me then pull the latch herself. Sheep are not stupid animals." I personally have known a few silly ones in my time as a vet, but I take his point.

Sheep have a rather undeserved reputation. One study found they could recognise and remember at least 50 different faces for more than two years after seeing them. That's longer than many people. Another study found sheep can learn how to complete tasks, such as navigating their way out of a complex maze. They also care for their young and can pick them out quickly, even when they are bunched together in a flock.

I often visit the Shaws' farm, and Philip has featured in *The Yorkshire Vet* a couple of times. One of those occasions was even shown on Channel 4's *Gogglebox*. It was when he was knocked over by a boisterous calf that seems to have been spooked by too many unfamiliar faces. Luckily, Philip was unhurt. "Grandad's on his arse again" is how one of his grandchildren put it, but nothing was dented, apart, perhaps, from Philip's pride. It's the kind of unexpected incident you have to get used to on a farm, although not all of them are funny. A few months ago I did mouth-to-mouth resuscitation at Philip's place on two lambs who, after making their entrance into the world, were struggling to stay here. I arrived in the middle of the night and managed to ease them out of their mother even though they had become dangerously tangled up inside. But once out, neither drew a breath. I rubbed them both briskly then breathed air into their lungs before they suddenly sparked into life.

"The kiss of life," said Philip, beaming.

"I'd rather do it on an animal than a human," I replied with a grin.

There we were, two grey-haired men, shattered from fatigue and stress, but over the moon that we'd managed to keep these two lambs alive. Sadly, one of them died soon afterwards, but I'd tried my best. Philip knew that.

Over a cup of tea in Philip's cosy farmhouse living room not long ago, I learned more about how he acquired the knowledge to succeed in his second career. He'd already known a fair bit about cattle from his childhood, but knew next to nothing about sheep. He studied at agricultural college, but most of what he knows he's gleaned through listening to and watching the experts.

"The man we bought our land from in Shropshire was a wonderful stockman in his 80s. He was a great help with the cows," said Philip, as he slurped his tea.

At least I could hear him. Outside I'd been struggling to catch his words, as his Call Ducks were making a racket. These are small, domesticated ducks, thought to have originally come from Asia. Because of their distinctive cry, they were often used by hunters to attract wild ducks towards traps. The Call Ducks would be tethered nearby and left to do what they do best: call out. The sound – rather like a cackle of laughter – would draw the other ducks to their doom.

There are some Call Ducks near my own home too. Like Philip, I cackle back at them if they dare to laugh at me when I'm working up a sweat in my garden.

Philip was beginning to sidetrack – he does that a lot – and I laughed as he told me about a mutual friend's close shave on a tractor. Its heavy trailer tipped over while he helped Philip to clear away a load of cow's muck. The trailer was badly damaged but luckily the cab – and in it our frightened mate – remained upright, propped up by an ancient hedge. Countless hedges have been cut down to make way for huge tractors and bigger fields but this one had remained, a sanctuary for wildlife as well as a lifesaver for a human being. Just then the Shaws' 11-year-old little rescue dog Willow, who had been sitting contentedly on Janet's lap, began to yap at some lambs she'd spotted through the window, and the sight of them took Philip back to his original tale.

"So after we'd bought the land in Shropshire we happened to find a shepherd in the village who'd just retired," he said. What luck. The shepherd was about 70 and had spent 50 years working with a flock of 500. "He was walking around with a sheepdog and no sheep."

With all this expert advice, plus their own drive and passion for country life, it was onwards and upwards for the Shaws. Their first lamb, Blackie, went off to market in Shropshire in the back of their estate car, but only after Janet and the staff in her grocery shop had said a tearful goodbye. The Shaws soon moved back to Yorkshire, and they clearly love it. How could they not? Where they live is idyllic – snowdrops and bluebells galore in the spring, stunning views in all four seasons. And although Philip is not as obviously soft with his animals as Steve and Jeanie Green ("Since the business with

Blackie, we don't name our animals," he said), it's obvious farming was always in his blood; it just took him a little time to start doing what he was born to do.

Another one of the experts to have helped him along is the late Will Burdett, a leading breeder of hens who, in his time, won many awards for his prize birds.

I met Will once or twice in the 1980s when I was a newly qualified vet. He would occasionally come to the practice at Kirkgate with a sick hen; most needed treatment for respiratory diseases and Donald leapt on such cases, being a bird fanatic. Philip first met Will in the spring of 1999, a few weeks after moving back up north. He wanted to buy some Orpington hens and was told one of the world's top experts – Will – was a neighbour. Orpington hens are majestic birds: plump and colourful and attractive. They are known as good egg layers and all that flesh provides tasty meat. Philip knocked on Will's door and asked if he could buy three chicks, but Will told him to come back later. Philip kept popping back, but Will kept putting him off. It was only later he realised that the hen breeder was waiting to see how the chicks developed – so he could keep the best for himself – before allowing any of them to leave the coop.

Over time Philip and Will became friends, and soon Philip was helping the older man out with plumbing and heating issues, and the odd bit of gardening. Will slowly opened up, regaling Philip with helpful information about hens as well as other interesting tales. "He looked after the Queen Mother's hens for years," said Philip. "Her equerry used to arrive to take them to shows; Will sometimes had to go along to present the birds. There were photos in his house of him and the Queen Mother and they often spoke on the phone. He was really upset when she died." Will was awarded an MBE in 2005, three years after the Queen Mother's death, and went to Buckingham Palace to collect it. It's odd to think of her keeping hens. For some reason, I just cannot imagine her poking around looking for eggs for her breakfast.

The friendship that developed between Will and Philip nicely highlights the community spirit I grew up with. It's reassuring when people know their neighbours and look out for one another. When Will was poorly and considering giving up his hens, Philip took one of the old man's incubators with some eggs to another breeder nearby, where they hatched. Later, when Will was feeling better but unsure about whether or not to continue with his hens, Philip persuaded him to give it another go, then went to collect the young birds on his behalf. "Will turned the heat lamps on and got everything ready, including the show cages with their baths and showers. When I went back later on to see how he was getting on, there they all were, Will and the hens, chatting away; they brought him back to life." Towards the end of Will's life, when he was struggling to walk even the 150 yards to his main hen house, Philip put garden chairs along this short route so he could take a rest every now and then.

Ultimately, old age caught up with Will. By then in his 90s, he told Philip he wanted rid of all his hens. Sadly, some were killed by a mink shortly afterwards, but Will did travel to Birmingham for one last show with four of his best birds. He even won another award. Back home, the two men put green rings on the legs of Will's remaining hens. "Now we know which are yours and which are mine," Philip told him. "I'll take them home for now, but when you are feeling better I will bring them back to you."

The birds never made it back home, as Will died not long afterwards, but his legacy happily lives on at Philip's farm. I can literally see and hear it, strutting and squawking in the Yorkshire dirt. Philip Shaw encapsulates much of what is good about farming in Yorkshire. He cares about the land and his animals and the people around him. Farming for him is not just a job. It's a calling.

The Banks family in the vegetable garden at The Black Swan, Oldstead, one of the world's best restaurants according to TripAdvisor – just six miles from Thirsk.

CHAPTER 4

Eat, Drink and Be Merry...

It pays to have a serious attitude when it comes to what we eat in Yorkshire. I've always known the county produces some of the best food you can put into your mouth, but even I was surprised when a restaurant run by an old schoolmate and distant relative was named the world's best fine dining establishment. Not just the best in Yorkshire or in Britain, but the best in the world.

The accolade was bestowed by TripAdvisor, the US travel and restaurant website that rates the places we stay and eat. It apparently collected and collated reviews over a 12-month period and then came up with the best. I was gobsmacked when I heard they had chosen The Black Swan in the village of Oldstead. This is what the restaurant says about itself: "Guests experience something unique – an intimate reflection of our character, our place and our lives". I couldn't have put it better myself. Mind you, be prepared to wait a bit if you want to eat there. The pub was popular before, but now you sometimes have to wait more than two months to get a weekend table. I suppose we have journalists to blame for that. They descended on the Black Swan in droves when the restaurant won its award. Sky News and the BBC were there; their crews set up at opposite ends of the dining room. It was even featured on US television.

The Black Swan, which is also a bed and breakfast, is a family concern whose head is a man called Tom Banks. He's a fourth-generation Yorkshire farmer and definitely someone who's willing to try new things. I rarely see him nowadays, but when I was a teenager I knew him well. He's the younger brother of Manda, my first girlfriend, and we all went to the same secondary school in Thirsk. I often stayed at the Banks' farm, which once belonged to Byland Abbey. Now a glorious ruin, the abbey, just up the road from the farm, was one of the great monasteries of England, although when I was a teenager I didn't pay it much attention. I was busy studying and enjoying myself, although I do remember that Manda and I sometimes ground corn to make our own flour for bread. Perhaps the spirit of food adventure has always been in the family.

Tom and his wife Anne live on the farm he grew up on; he only really left to study at agricultural college for three years near York. With their two grown-up sons, chef Tommy and front-of-house-man James, the couple now run the restaurant. They are doing so well they've opened a second one in York. The restaurants are just the latest links in a chain that begins with the Banks' farm, first taken over by Tom's grandfather, who was also called Tom (the name is a family tradition). Old Tom was given the land rent-free for seven years after the First World War, when the country was trying to get back on its feet and agriculture needed a boost. It was a tough life and there wasn't much of a living to be earned. But old Tom seemed like a man who could make a success of such circumstances; he was what would now be described as a character.

In the 1920s, he killed a barn owl with a walking stick; it had been eating his chicks. He had the owl stuffed and it's still in the farmhouse to this day, staring down at anyone going up and down the stairs with its unseeing eyes. The old farmer once insisted that a story included in one of the Herriot books was about him. Alf, the vet-turned-author, who knew the Banks family well, usually altered names and places to try to avoid identifying people, but this strategy didn't always work. In this particular tale he wrote about a large goose going berserk at a farm while the hapless Herriot looked on. Suddenly, the farmer grabbed the bird and chucked it through a hatch, up into a granary, to get it out the way.

"No, the story is not about you," Alf had said when old Tom accused him of using his story for material.

"It was!" insisted the farmer, intent on getting to the truth, or what he believed was the truth, like a dog with a bone. "D'you mean to say someone else 'as done *that*? 'As chucked an old goose like *that*?!" It was a good point.

Those Herriot years are gone. The Banks' 160-acre farm is still there, but run on very different lines. Three quarters of the land is potentially arable and crops like wheat and barley used to be grown. There were also some beef cattle. But now there are no crops or cattle; Tom got rid of his last cows in the 1990s after the outbreak of Mad Cow Disease. Most of the land these days is left wild, which is definitely good news for wildlife; the distinctive call of the owl can be regularly heard, although Tom is considering buying some cattle again to produce meat for the family's two restaurants, the focus of much of what now goes on at the farm. He is even thinking of planting a vineyard, because global warming continues to change the climate of Yorkshire.

The restaurant operation has 80 or so staff, some of them full-time gardeners who grow food that is fed to diners. Much of what is on the menu is produced on the farm but some of it is even closer to hand: there is a two-acre vegetable plot right outside The Black Swan. Its garden's terraces were created with 500 tons of soil brought over from Tom's farmland. All sorts are grown from lavender, strawberries and blackcurrants to kale, sprouts and cucumbers. Chefs are known to shoot out from the small kitchen, running past bewildered diners to grab the freshest produce possible from the garden. Sweetcorn is best eaten shortly after it's picked – preferably within 20 minutes. At The Black Swan the vegetable appears on the plate, often in a light filo pastry, in no time at all. Tom said getting food from ground to table as quickly as possible is part of the theatre of the restaurant.

I remember Tom was a big fan of his mother's roast beef and Yorkshire puddings, but he's now devoted to producing far more exotic produce, such as crapaudine beetroot. It's lovely to see his passion. Crapaudine roughly translates as female toad in French. It's called that because the skin is like a toad's. "It's an ugly beetroot," said Tom, sitting in the restaurant's dark and atmospheric 17th-century bar one rainy afternoon. Most farmers in their right mind wouldn't grow this version of the vegetable, as it can be difficult to cultivate. But Tom thinks it's worth all the hard work. Beetroot cooked in beef fat (it's named "Crapaudine Beetroot cooked in Beef Fat" on the menu, a blunt Yorkshire explanation, describing exactly what you're eating) is one of the restaurant's signature dishes. People who don't even like beetroot have been won over. There are other uncommon ingredients too, including chicory and artichoke. The latter is another vegetable Tom is passionate about; he even made an artichoke-connected culinary discovery. One day he was gently simmering artichoke juice in his farmhouse kitchen when the telephone rang. He chatted for a little longer than expected and when he came back saw the syrup he was trying to make had turned into a toffee-like substance. Determined not to waste what he'd made, he tasted it and realised it was delicious. The proof was, quite literally, in the pudding; now his artichoke 'fudge' is served as petits fours, miniature sweet treats.

Like many families in the 1960s and 70s, including my own, the Bankses were interested in food, and have always been able to enjoy a lot of fresh and local produce in their rural setting. There was, of course, far less choice when Tom and I were children with little, if any, processed food. Our parents and grandparents grew a lot of things; we all knew what we were eating and where it came from, as we had often helped to plant and harvest it ourselves.

There are still many people who get excited about growing their own food, or are at least interested in growing some; there are thousands of people on allotment waiting lists. But it's a shame some children don't know how carrots and potatoes come into existence. Some only really find out where their vegetables come from during school trips to places like the 240-acre Stirley Farm near Huddersfield. Now owned by the Yorkshire Wildlife Trust, it's run by a few staff, with the help of volunteers. Some even learn how to look after cattle – the farm produces delicious beef. Visiting children have been able to get stuck in, digging up vegetables, cooking them in the kitchen of a converted barn, and eating what they've prepared. It's brilliant, and an excellent antidote to the grim knowledge that some youngsters think cheese comes from plants! Tom is now trying, in his small way, to recreate the forgotten past. He said he was missing out all the middlemen – the supermarkets, the wholesalers – who, he believed, have a stranglehold on UK farming. "They stop customers paying the right price for food," he explained. At the restaurant no one other than family or staff are involved in the decision-making. "We decide what to sow, then sow it, and put it in the kitchen for the chefs to cook," said Tom. "I come in and see the smiles on the faces of the people who have eaten our food. It's very fulfilling." The restaurant's style is to use the very best ingredients, wasting very little through pickling and fermenting and a tasting menu that allows just about everything to be used. The team also experiments with different flavours and recipes, and it's so successful that people are queuing up to eat in the quaint pub. Even many of the tables that diners eat off are handmade at the farm.

The Black Swan shows just how far Yorkshire and Britain have come. Nearly gone are the days when our cuisine was laughed at; when we were renowned for soggy steak and kidney puddings, greasy fish and chips and cholesterol-ridden fry-ups. It is possible to eat like a king on British food, although with the Black Swan's prices, it's fair to say that a meal there is only for special treats – but well worth saving up for.

Celebrating Yorkshire's finest food and drink is an increasingly popular activity, and one I'm proud to be associated with. The Great Yorkshire Show is one of many places where my county and its people can show off their latest creations each year. Although I rarely visited the show as a child – Harrogate seemed a very long way from Thirsk back then. Now I go most years, often filmed for TV.

Friends compete against friends there, and it's always fun to see their excitement and nerves beforehand and afterwards, when the tension is relieved with a few pints. I've been surrounded by animals all my life, but still find the event fascinating. And, just like in the veterinary world, there is always something you don't expect.

For the 2019 show, internationally recognised sculptor Emma Stothard, from Hull, created an impressive willow and wire installation modelled on hens, fruit and vegetables. But at the 160th show last year she went one better, managing to recreate the Craven Heifer, a giant beast of a cow that found fame in the early 19th century because of her enormous frame. The cow was reared on the Duke of Devonshire's estate at Bolton Abbey in the Yorkshire Dales, and was deliberately fattened up to create a monster. She weighed more than 170 stone and stood taller than 7ft. She was apparently so big that a special door, twice as wide as usual, was constructed so she could get in and out of the cowshed. If I had been her vet I would have ensured she went on a diet; I don't like to see obesity in animals. But two centuries ago attitudes were a bit different. When this humongous heifer travelled to London's Smithfield Market she stopped off at towns along the way, where she would draw large appreciative crowds. She is still the largest cow ever shown in England.

Sculptor Emma, now based in Whitby, recreated the Craven Heifer in steel. It even had the animal's famous brown and white markings. Emma started her career with a loan from the Prince's Trust, and made the Prince of Wales a large-scale portrait of his Jack Russell dog Tigga from willow grown on Prince Charles' Highgrove Estate. She gave it to him as a thank you gift. At the Great Yorkshire Show Emma's steel cow, lovingly made in Yorkshire, was adored by the public. It popped up at locations across the county before arriving at the showground. It's probably been in more selfies than I have – and it has the added advantage of not being prone to blink as the shutter clicks or say silly things, as I sometimes do.

As I said, there's always something unexpected happening at the Great Yorkshire Show. My TV colleague Julian Norton and

I amazed ourselves – and our wives – strutting our stuff on the catwalk for the first time a couple of years ago to show off the latest tweed clothes from the Yorkshire Agricultural Society. Another first for a country bumpkin who's more often than not covered in muck, and I did it again this year. The pair of us, along with the Greens, have also taken part in Countryside Live. It's in a similar vein to the Great Yorkshire Show, and takes place each October at the Harrogate showground. I've found myself doing question and answer sessions there about The Yorkshire Vet to a huge crowd. I'm getting used to this kind of thing now, but still find it rather nerve-wracking. As Herriot might have said, these things shouldn't happen to a vet. But they do.

Despite the nerves, I'm always proud to promote Yorkshire and the food we produce here; it's becoming increasingly prominent. It's certainly a treat to be given so many opportunities to try fantastic local fare, and not just at farmers' markets. At the Great Yorkshire Show a couple of years ago, Julian and I met entrepreneurs Toby and Jane Whittaker. They were filmed for The Yorkshire Vet and we sampled some of their gin. They began selling it in the summer of 2015 when their business was still tiny; their first order was for just 24 bottles. The gin was initially created in two small stills, both called Jezebel, that were placed in a converted pig shed near their remote Nidderdale farmhouse. The couple now turn over around half a million pounds a year; that's about 25,000 bottles. What an achievement in such a short space of time!

It's a particularly impressive feat given that neither of them has a background in production or farming. Toby did a chemistry degree, but hadn't used it in more than two decades. Now he's in his element in his mini-lab with its big stainless steel worktops, surrounded by stills, tanks and countless half-full "test" bottles. It looks a little like a school chemistry lab. He tries out various recipes before he and Jane are happy that the result is as close to perfection as possible. What the Whittakers are doing on their 54 acres, up a long farm track close to the River Nidd and the village of Dacre, is clearly working. Their gins, each with a hare on the label, sell in Britain and abroad.

The couple are animal mad and have horses, dogs, and chickens. They use local ingredients whenever they can. "We want to keep things traditional and identify with the area," said Jane, who Toby describes as a great cook. But it isn't always possible to stick to even British suppliers, let alone ones from Yorkshire. Juniper, for example, is a key ingredient in gin, but the Whittakers mostly get theirs from Macedonia. As Jane said: "English junipers are not particularly good for gin making, as they have too much moisture. They have to be grown in a high-temperature climate."

Many other raw materials are sourced in Britain, though, including bilberries, mulberries, hawthorne berries and bog myrtle. Some come from Yorkshire, some from Sussex and Scotland. One gin recipe uses honey from just up the road, but there are plans to source it from even nearer: the Whittakers want a beehive on their own farm. Jane already grows thyme in the garden and has planted fruit trees. Some of the fruit ends up in a gin or two. The finished product is poured into bottles from Allied Glass – in Leeds.

Initially interested in making beer, Toby signed up to a Masters course in brewing and distilling, and got planning permission for a microbrewery before he and Jane decided they should actually set up a distillery and make their own gin. Like many people, they both enjoy a drink, which I suppose helps. Now the Whittakers have eight stills, most of them holding about 330 litres. Some were made in Tadcaster in Yorkshire specially for the firm. This year the couple built a brand new bigger distillery, complete with a shop for tourists and those who want to taste the products. London's Fortnum and Mason and Yorkshire stately home Harewood House are among the firm's customers in the UK, and Hong Kong and Macau have started to import Whittaker's gin too. It's even sent to Switzerland.

Jane and Toby hope to tap into the US, perhaps starting with Colorado, where they went skiing and got chatting to someone in their hotel where they were staying who agreed to let them send him a few bottles. In such ways do our small companies grow large. The Whittakers have now even decided to branch out into beer and whisky. It takes at least three years to make the latter. Of course, they plan to use barley grown right here in Yorkshire.

Barley, berries and bottles are a long way from their previous jobs in property, but Jane and Toby seem to have successfully bridged the gap. Making gin is something they have both come to relatively late in life. After meeting on a blind date they decided they also wanted to work together and do something creative. Yorkshire gin was, quite literally, their solution.

While Jane is a southerner, she says she far prefers Yorkshire and its countryside to the south. Her love affair with her adopted county is clear to see. Toby grew up near Leeds before moving as a child to the countryside not far from his current home, although he was sent away to school. Now he's making up for lost time, and can't get enough of Nidderdale.

The couple live and work next to fields of sheep and horses. In the spring the nearby church has a blanket of nodding daffodils leading up to its door and a charming wooden shelter made by local children for hedgehogs. It's been lovingly stuffed with straw and is known as The Hedgehog Hilton.

A few miles from the Whittakers' distillery is the almost painfully picturesque village of Ripley. There's a hotel there called the Boar's Head that was opened in 1990 by a vicar who blessed the pumps. It was a significant event, as before that Ripley is thought to have been dry for 71 years because of the opposition of the local aristocrat, Sir William Ingilby. A former priest, he ordered all three village pubs to close on Sundays, the most lucrative day of trading. In response, they completely closed their doors. Now, a few miles from what was an alcohol no-go zone, you can sample gin and tonics with the Whittakers. What would Sir William have made of that I wonder? Probably not much. But it works for me. The Whittakers, though, despite their passion for gin, are careful not to overdo it, and are very health-conscious. They eat less meat nowadays, and what they do eat is bought from the butcher, not the supermarket. Jane says their waistlines, and the environment, are the better for the change.

"And if we want a gin and tonic, we only have one after 6pm," says Toby. "If I drank any earlier I wouldn't be able to concentrate. So 6pm it is, and not a moment before." I'll drink to that.

I'll also happily drink to the Flavours of Herriot Country Awards, another foodie event that's becoming the toast of the town, in Yorkshire at least. The aim is to celebrate the best in food, drink and hospitality on Herriot's old stomping ground. Alf Wight loved his food, both British and foreign. He'd have been delighted to see Yorkshire produce doing so well, and pleased his books have done something to promote it. He often wrote about the delicious fare he'd eaten, whichever unusual situation he happened to find himself in. He wrote with pleasure about the food he'd once had on board a ship transporting sheep to the Soviet Union, where he'd been hired to check on the animals. It was mouth-watering stuff: "The cook produced what I think must have been a banquet in my honour, because it had a touch of England about it. A delectable soup of celery, spinach and other vegetables, then roast pork with crackling accompanied by roast ham, potatoes and red cabbage. Dessert was sago pudding thickly sprinkled with cinnamon." Just reading those lines makes me peckish.

CHAPTER 5

A View of Life from Sutton Bank

I t was a cold and damp February morning, and my head was foggy with a lack of sleep – and a lack of breakfast – but I forgot everything when Midnight in Havana and Pepys suddenly thundered past. The sight and sound of these magnificent racehorses, so close I could almost touch their gleaming flanks, left me feeling elated and grateful to be alive. The animals and their jockeys had no sooner flown by than I turned my head to see two more horses and their riders pelting full throttle in my direction. They seemed to accelerate as they advanced. I found out later that one was called Helovaplan – he was certainly a hell of a sight.

I was standing on a piece of flat green land known as the gallops, near trainer Bryan Smart's 17th-century house and stables. The area is an out-of-the-way spot at the top of Sutton Bank, a high point in the Hambleton Hills about 1,000ft above sea level, right on the edge of the Yorkshire Moors. It's used to train horses. They have been running up here for about four centuries, on what's believed to have been one of the country's earliest racecourses. I'd wager there were some interesting bets. Hambleton was apparently known as the second Newmarket, with the Gold Cup one of the best prizes. It was a four-mile race and was perhaps the forerunner of the prestigious

Ascot Gold Cup. The racecourse was at its height in the 17th and 18th centuries, but then went into decline. The racing eventually went to Yorkshire's other courses, at Thirsk, York and Ripon. But the area is still used for training.

Although I've lived in the area for most of my life, I'd never seen horses running up there before. And now here I was, with a single white, waist-height railing the only thing separating me from them. I was in awe of the spectacle I was witnessing, even if there was little time to enjoy it given the horses' speed. (The fact I hadn't paid to watch also appealed; sometimes there is such a thing as a free lunch.) I was standing on what is basically a smaller, shorter version of a "real" track, designed to allow the animals to run in all weathers and get a feel for the real thing. Normally about 40 horses are exercised by Bryan's team each day. It was only 9.15am, but there had already been two other sessions that particular morning.

Bryan was by my side, full of banter and chitchat as usual. But he was very much focused on the horses. Pepys, he explained, had won six races and twice come in second, while Helovaplan "might run on Friday. He's won two races and was third in his last run at Newcastle." It was a challenge to keep up with all the different horses. But Bryan knows each animal's pedigree, personality and past performance like the back of his hand. He can reel off their unique quirks, walks and injuries, even though he and wife Vicky, an equine sports therapist, have 50 to 60 horses at their stables, sometimes more. Some are owned by the ruler of Dubai's son or businessmen based in the Persian Gulf. With a staff of about 15, it is a big operation, but also a way of life.

I'd arrived an hour or so earlier, popping in for a chat and a cup of coffee on my day off, enjoying a little interlude travelling around my own backyard. The couple's home and stables are just a few miles from my place. I'd travelled down country lanes much of the way, before climbing Sutton Bank's steep hairpin bend followed by another muddy track. The route is soothing and familiar; I've probably driven this way more often than I've eaten roast beef and Yorkshire pudding, which is saying something.

I've known the Smarts for a while, although I don't deal with them professionally; horse racing has its own specialist vets. But I know their stables very well. The man who owned it before them was another horse trainer, called Jack Calvert. As I drove into the Smarts' yard his name popped into my mind. I knew his next-door neighbour too, a man by the name of Joe Carr. I smiled fleetingly, thinking about the two elderly men before I remembered and my heart sank. Joe and Jack were both dead, with other people now sipping tea and eating cornflakes in their old kitchens. A trainer called Kevin Ryan has Joe's place now; I drove past Kevin's sign on my way to the Smarts.

I have visited both of these stables at the top of Sutton Bank a number of times over the years, although not nearly as often as my old boss Donald Sinclair, a horse fanatic and expert. He, like Joe Carr, was also a pigeon fancier; the two men were race rivals, but friends too. Donald often visited the gallops and sometimes I'd tag along. Horses frequently needed two vets back then, when anaesthetics weren't nearly as reliable as they are now. I also occasionally went by myself, perhaps to deal with a case of horse colic.

I hadn't been up to the gallops for quite a while, but I was here on a pre-arranged social call and Vicky came out to meet me when I pulled up. We chatted as we walked into the warm and cosy kitchen, masses of horse photographs and rosettes for the Smarts and their showjumping daughter on the walls and shelves. The family's little dog, Toffee, waddled up to me for a brief sniff and I saw Bryan quickly finishing his cereal and pushing his bowl away. He was pleased to see me, but his smile didn't last long. As Vicky poured me a coffee he received a phone call that instantly changed his mood. "Oh, you're joking," he barked into the phone. After a brief chat he ended the call and then let loose.

"They're now saying they'll not allow any runners if they haven't been vaccinated in the last six months. Ridiculous. We've already been done for the year." Bryan apologised for getting heated, but he really didn't need to. Nor did he need to fill me in on the background; I knew exactly what he was talking about. The horse racing industry had been closed down for several days because of an outbreak of equine flu. It had begun at a trainer's yard in Cheshire; soon more than 100 stables were in lockdown and races suspended while the authorities struggled to contain the contagious illness.

The disease is rarely fatal, but because horses move around a lot for races it can quickly infect thousands of animals. Symptoms, sometimes persisting for weeks, include fever, coughing and nasal discharge, with an incubation period of one to five days. Vaccinated horses can be infected too, even if they don't show many or any symptoms. I'd already advised one client who runs a pony club to sit tight and see how the situation developed, keeping any animal with symptoms separate from the rest. For the Smarts, whose lives and livelihood centre on racing and horses, the flu outbreak was a serious setback, even though none of their animals were ill.

The February outbreak came just a few weeks before the start of the Cheltenham Festival, which is followed by Aintree and the Grand National. The whole industry, worth billions to the economy and employing thousands of people had, at that point in time, ground to a halt. There had not been such a shutdown since the 2001 foot-and-mouth crisis. As it turned out, the British Horseracing Authority would soon allow racing to begin again, albeit with strict controls. But my visit to the Smarts came at the height of the outbreak and it naturally worried them.

Once our discussion about flu, vaccines and animal welfare had run its course, Bryan offered to take me out to see a few of the horses. We passed several in the yard, including the four I would see on the gallops a few minutes later. As the horses' hooves clattered on the cobbles, Bryan gave a couple of last-minute instructions to their jockeys before we climbed into a jeep and bounced off over the grass to the nearby training area. On the way he told me how his love of horses had diverted him from a life underground. He grew up in a village near Barnsley and his father, like most men in that area at that time, was a miner. Sons then usually followed in the footsteps of their fathers, but when Bryan was seven he did something that would set him on a different course. His parents went on a trip with a working men's club to York Races, which is ironic considering what followed. Bryan didn't go; his cousin Linda was roped in to look after him. She took him with her to a stable nearby where she had a lesson. "That was it," said Bryan. "I knew from that moment that I had to work with horses; they get in your blood."

To be fair, Bryan already had an inkling of what was to come. From an early age he had an affinity with pit ponies, sometimes riding them around fields with no saddle and a bridle made of string. He began taking his granny's beer bottles to the pub where he exchanged them for cash, money that he put to good use. "Mum let me have one riding lesson every week. Granny's bottles paid for it," Bryan said, as we pulled up near the track and got out of his jeep. His parents eventually bought him a pony called Morgan for £65, and he hooked up with a nearby dealer who took him on the northern showjumping circuit, where he also learned to ride other horses and ponies. "I loved going fast," he told me with a grin, just before four horses thundered by us. I couldn't really relate; while I like horses, I didn't enjoy the riding lessons I took in my 20s. I'd much rather be injecting or stitching a horse than pelting along on its back.

On our way back to the yard I heard more about Bryan. He was born in 1956, just days before me. At 15 he could barely read or write (he later found out he was dyslexic), but managed to make out some of the words in a Horse & Hound advert. A head lad was wanted to work with "sick, lame and lazy racehorses" for Jenny Pitman, then a trainer just starting out, now a novelist. His mum wrote an application letter for him and after an interview showing off his horsemanship skills, Bryan got the job. Before he left school to take up the post, the headmaster told him he'd never have a successful career in horses.

Jenny was the first woman to train a Grand National winner, and young Bryan rode several victorious horses for her as an amateur before turning professional. It was exciting to hear him describe his first win, while we sat in his jeep near his very own racing stables. "I rode Road Race, beating a horse called Sir Kay that had won his previous six outings. My instructions were to follow Sir Kay. Wherever Sir Kay goes, you go. So I did, and I won." And, what's better, he showed his former headmaster how wrong he had been.

Many other successes followed on around 200 winners, but it ended badly with a nasty fall in 1982. Bryan broke his foot, leg, and skull – and was lucky to survive. He moved into training, and has been doing well ever since. "There's more pleasure in training a winner than riding," he told me. As we walked through his yard, past several horses moving slowly forward in a circular walker, I thought about how he and Vicky were from quite different backgrounds. Her rather refined voice contrasts with Bryan's Yorkshire accent. She used to work with Lord Huntingdon, who trained some of the Queen's horses. But that's all irrelevant. What counts is the fact that their shared interest in horses brought them together. And it's clear they care for their animals very well. They even have a jacuzzi and a solarium for them, lucky things.

Having watched some beautiful horses and chewed the fat with the Smarts, I felt the day was off to a fine start. I said my goodbyes and set off to see yet another horse not far away. It was a climb, although I tackled the steep bends easily – no problem at all in my modern car. It wasn't so easy for Alf in the 1930s and 40s, especially in bad weather, driving around in, say, a little Austin 7.

Jim, Alf's son, and I had that point hammered home when we drove the same make of car for the filming of a *Yorkshire Vet* special about the Herriot years. It took patience, not to mention time, to chug up the hills. I certainly wouldn't have fancied trying to drive up them in the snow in such a vehicle. I reached my destination quickly and after pulling up in a more or less empty car park, I realised I felt as if I'd come home. I'd been to this spot so many times before, first as a child, then as a teenager; my mates and I would often bike round here. Later, I came with my wife and children and our boxer dogs Bert and Alf. We came to walk and to look at a massive old horse, Britain's largest.

Just in case you haven't already guessed, this was no ordinary horse. It wasn't really a horse at all; just a silhouette of one cut into the hillside. I turned off the engine and sat at the steering wheel, peering out and up at this magnificent 318ft wide, 220ft high image, or at least the bit of it I could see through my windscreen. I couldn't take in the whole thing because it covers about an acre. Munching on a peanut butter sandwich, I marvelled anew at her size and thought about the people who fashioned her from the soil in 1857. Queen Victoria was on the throne at the time, and still a young woman.

The Kilburn White Horse was the idea of businessman Thomas Taylor. He was from the nearby village of Kilburn, but had gone to work in London. Seeing horse shapes cut into various inclines down south, he was inspired to make one on his home turf. John Hodgson, Kilburn's schoolmaster and a practising surveyor in his spare time, declared it all possible. Money was then raised and the project was funded through a donation from Thomas and a public appeal. With the help of some of his pupils, John marked out the figure of a horse on the contours of the hillside, before a group of local men stepped up to help remove the turf and deposit several tons of lime on top. An ancestor of Manda Banks, my first girlfriend, was one of the schoolboys involved in the project.

The very sharp minds among you might wonder why they had to put lime on the horse. It's because most hillside horses are cut into chalk and so are naturally white. The Kilburn horse, though, was cut into sandstone and therefore needs regular artificial whitening. It was often whitened with lime or chalk chippings and, in later years, even spruced up with a touch of masonry paint. That's why referring to it as a white horse is something of a misnomer. It often looks grey; in fact, its local nickname is "the old grey mare" and it needs constant attention to keep it looking bright. The only time we didn't want it to shine out was during the Second World War, when it had to be covered over so it wouldn't act as a navigational guide for German bombers.

As a pensioner in 1921, Manda's ancestor was asked to give his thoughts on how and why the horse he helped construct decades before was made in the first place. He wrote a poem that might not have won any awards for its composition, but certainly captures the mood of the time. Part of it talks about how the teacher Mr Hodgson:

> *Called out John Rowley, biggest of the lot,*
> *Saying, "Will you come and help me to measure out the plot?"*
> *The work was very hard, but with great skill and care*
> *The master and the youth both tried to do their share*
> *And other boys as well were glad to pull the chain*
> *And help the Master in his work preparing for the men.*

The poem continued:

> *Then thirty-one men of Kilburn accustomed to the spade*
> *Went to work right heartily and soon the plot was bared.*
> *Although it was so difficult they managed it quite well*
> *For only one man had a fall and rolled right down the hill.*
> *But soon as they saw he was not hurt it caused a lot of mirth*
> *When an avalanche of sods came down which pinned him to the earth.*

It might not be Wordsworth, but we get the idea.

As far as I know, the poor chap who rolled down the hill was none the worse for his ordeal, and the village's white horse was soon finished, bringing visitors flocking to the area to see it. There is an interesting footnote to the accident, though. For decades the horse was looked after by a troop of volunteers, but a couple of years ago, responsibility for the maintenance was passed to the Forestry Commission. They decided it was too dangerous for volunteers to have to cling to the hillside while they carried out their work. Apparently, workers with specialist equipment were needed. Health and safety, eh. In fact, the rules are now so tight that people can't actually sit on the horse as they used to do.

I used to walk in the Sutton Bank area a lot with Alf and his dogs and, although I never visited the white horse with him, I tend to think of him when I am there. That's partly because the last thing he wrote, three days before his death, was the foreword to a booklet about the White Horse Association, the charity that maintained the horse. In it, Alf described the thrill of his very first sight of the huge creature. "It is something which has remained with me over the years," he said.

I got out of my car and climbed the 151 steps to the top of the horse, putting thoughts about its colour and my old boss to the back of my mind. The steps are quite steep and as I'd been busy with work I'd let myself get out of shape a little, so I was out of breath when I reached the summit. I wasn't in the best of moods when I arrived, because on the way up I noticed a little black sack full of dog turds lying on the ground. I muttered to myself and inwardly swore. Why hadn't the dog owner taken the mess away with them? But I immediately forgot this negative line of thinking the moment I stood totally still and soaked up the view over the Vale of York towards the Pennines. It was windy and cold, but it blew the cobwebs away in an instant. I looked down and around at a sweeping green panorama as far as the eye could see. It was totally familiar, but as captivating as ever, although my feelings were tinged with a little sadness. I spotted a farm once owned by an ex-cavalry officer called Arthur Dand, a kind old man who I used to visit to look over his herd of cows. If, for some reason, I hadn't been able to save one of his animals, he'd just say: "Never mind. Come on in, 'ave a cup of tea." His home is now a water-bottling factory.

A quick chat with an elderly couple about the White Horse and who should look after it pulled me back to the present. I walked on a bit and saw below, in the distance, the village of Kilburn, which I know like the back of my hand. I smiled, remembering how I once stitched up a stallion's head there. Nothing surprising about that – the memorable bit was that I did it in a kitchen. We had to go inside as it was the middle of the night and too dark to see properly outside, even with a torch. Luckily the house, kitchen and doorways were all on the large side and the horse was a picture of serenity, despite his bloody gash. He stood still with barely a murmur, composed and calm, apparently taking in the crockery on the dresser and the washing up in the sink.

When I was a child, the three churches of Bagby, Thirkleby (where I lived) and Kilburn were run together. We were basically one community, and I'm still a part of it. For years, I've been a church sidesman in Kilburn, my duties including lighting candles, putting hymn numbers on the board, and doing readings. Kilburn church will always have a special place in my affections, as does the village itself. I actually can't hear its name without thinking of Robert Thompson, the famous woodcarver nicknamed the "Mouseman". His furniture has probably done more to make Kilburn famous than the white horse. He made everything by hand, adding a small mouse to each item as a kind of signature. I never met him; he died in 1955, the year before I was born. Alf knew him, though. He was his vet, and told a lovely story about Robert, by then an old man with a white moustache, popping into our old practice in Kirkgate one day with his sick dog. But it wasn't his pet that was uppermost in his mind. Alf remembered the Mouseman standing in the dining room while he waited, gazing at a sideboard of French oak. It had been in Alf's wife's family for generations. Robert stood there entranced, stroking the wood and murmuring how beautiful it was.

He was born in Kilburn in 1876, the son of the village carpenter and joiner. He initially started working as an engineer's apprentice, but he also began to take a keen interest in medieval woodcarvings in Ripon cathedral. He returned home to work as a carpenter when his father died, and became more and more fascinated by English oak and medieval woodwork. Soon he started taking commissions. News of his skills began to travel and his work became sought after. He eventually employed around 30 people to help him. It's said he chose a mouse as his trademark because he remembered when he was as poor as a church mouse. It turned out to be a good emblem.

Ampleforth Abbey, the private Catholic school not far away, was one of Robert's early customers. In the 1920s the school decided to enlarge its Victorian library and Robert was asked to furnish it. He did a lot of other work there too, but the library is said by some to be his greatest achievement. People can visit the college and take a Church Mouse Tour. If they don't want to pay though, anyone interested in Robert's work can also visit Kilburn for nothing. The village church has the trademark mice carved onto the pews. They also feature on bars and furniture at the Forresters Arms pub, and there's Robert's 16th-century home to visit – or Mouseman's Cottage, as it's known. It's now a showroom for the company's furniture. And there's a workshop that people can see too. They can stand by a huge window at the top of some stairs to watch skilled craftsmen at work. There are also big piles of oak laid out in the elements. The wood is air-dried to minimise warping, before being shaped into beautiful items, from bedsteads and chests of drawers costing thousands of pounds to more affordable items like bookends and nut dishes. Each piece is finished off with a hand-carved mouse, craftsmen using the same hand tools the Mouseman used. Walt Disney said his empire started with a mouse – the same could be said about our Robert.

Of course, you can buy a piece of furniture in Kilburn, but items don't always come cheap. Older items are popular on the second-hand market, but they can cost a pretty penny too. In the 1930s the Mouseman and his team made office furniture for a new wing at the Horlick's factory in Slough, near London. Last year, one of the dressers sold at auction for an astonishing £35,000, while a refectory table went for £28,000. It's only furniture, one might say, but it's very attractive furniture, and made to last. Lin and I have a Mouseman lamp, milking stool, cheeseboard and bookends. They'll likely be in use and in pristine condition long after we've both gone.

It's amazing how a simple walk can bring on all these vivid mental pictures and memories. I'd been pondering Kilburn from my vantage point near the White Horse. Afterwards, my gaze shifted as I walked on under the huge and bright Yorkshire sky. My eyes and thoughts moved from the Mouseman and Kilburn to Hood Hill, a place where I like to stroll when I have an hour or two free.

Hundreds of years ago the wooded peak I was staring across at was the site of a castle. It's not hard to hazard a guess why the Normans chose that particularly spot for one of their many fortresses: Hood Hill offers a sweeping view of the surrounding countryside, and any potential enemies. Now, of course, it's walkers, not soldiers, who are

A sweeping green panorama... the view from Sutton bank over the Vale of York towards the Pennines, on a cold, windy day.

rewarded with a view of pretty fields of green. Cyclists can also follow a pleasant track along the bottom of the hill.

The old castle now is merely a group of banks, slopes, and ditches, its designers, builders and inhabitants long ago turned to dust. It's another reminder, if one were needed, of how fleeting and vulnerable we all are. Live life and try to enjoy it, I thought to myself.

Scanning the horizon not far from Hood Hill I stopped walking as I saw some more familiar sights: a couple of farms and also Janet Ferguson's place. A former dentist and one of my clients, she runs what I like to think of as a rest home for sheep in the grounds of her home. They are treated so well – Janet has even rigged up something that looks like a deckchair for the sheep to sit in while I clip their feet. They look for all the world like they're enjoying the sun on the beach at Scarborough.

As I walked on, remembering how I'd fallen over a few weeks ago while walking near Hood Hill, a man who recognised me from the television politely interrupted my reveries. He told me he enjoyed watching *The Yorkshire Vet*, so much so that he'd decided to bring his two dogs to the area from his home in Sheffield for a walk. Of course, he hadn't actually expected to bump into me. I was amused to see his pets, one slightly larger than the other. They were tethered together by a lead, and where one went the other had to go too. "If the big 'un runs off, the other one always brings him back," said the man.

It was time to go, I had another appointment, so began making my way back down the steps near the horse. I walked past a wooden bench bearing the dedication: Fred Banks, Guardian of the White Horse. He was a farmer and the father of my first girlfriend, Manda. He was also a man with many interests. He wrote about a lot of things, such as the monastic waterworks surrounding Byland Abbey and the history of Kilburn and the white horse. Fred was one of many involved in looking after the horse, and it's fitting that there's a commemorative bench for him right there. Fred was also involved in the Yorkshire Gliding Club, just a hop, skip and a jump from his bench; as a child he sometimes helped pull the ropes that launched the gliders over the cliff and into the air. That's where I was off to next.

I've flown in a glider from the club on Sutton Bank a couple of times before, including for my 60th birthday, which was filmed for *The Yorkshire Vet*. I enjoyed it, even though I struggled to overcome claustrophobia while cocooned in that small cockpit. I've told Lin, only half in jest, she could perhaps arrange to have my ashes flown around when I'm dead. It makes me chuckle to think of an urn full of what's left of me, strapped in and soaring above the land I love.

In 2015 the club made a super little film about its history, all set to music. I was both amused and bemused that a tune they used was taken from the 1990s blockbuster film *Titanic*. It seemed an odd choice given that we all know what happened to the ship. There's also some fabulous black and white footage in the video, showing smartly dressed men in the 1930s wearing jackets and ties. They'd have been among the very first to fly. In another scene one man, his back to the camera as he helps pull a glider from a shed, turns to reveal the pipe he's puffing on. Another man sits in a glider, a beret on his head and a cigarette hanging from his mouth. Different times indeed. But what was filmed from the air in those early days of black and white is more interesting still. There are superb shots of my old friend the white horse (she's certainly white in the film), as well as Lake Gormire, one of Alf's favourite places. It was formed thousands of years ago during the last ice age, when a glacier carved out the lake's bowl. Some say there's a submerged village in it.

Gliders were first launched from Sutton Bank at the dawn of aviation, and it's not hard to see why. The plateau suddenly gives way to a steep bank; gliders can simply be hurled off the edge. But the club as we know it now was started in 1934 by a group of pioneering aviators who cut the first proper runway into a patch of heather moorland.

In those early years the club had some famous names, such as Fred Slingsby, a First World War airman. He won the Military Medal for an extraordinary piece of skill. He was a gunner in a two-man plane that was carrying out a mission over enemy lines. When his pilot was killed, Fred climbed out of his gun position and into the cockpit, before getting the plane back home. He went on to build and fly gliders.

A world-famous aviator associated with the club was Hull's Amy Johnson. I would have loved to meet her. She was already an experienced pilot when she glided over Yorkshire and in 1930 she became the first woman to fly solo from England to Australia. She made other record-breaking flights too. Many club visitors enjoy looking at a framed letter from her that's been hung up on the club's café wall. It's dated August 1939 and tells how she was resigning from the club because she was moving down south. It didn't turn out well for Amy, though. Sadly, she died in early 1941 when her plane crashed in the Thames estuary. Her body was never found.

Nowadays, the gliding club has about 275 full flying members, as well as 30 or so juniors. Children can go up on their own at just 14 if they have had enough lessons. It seems strange that they are allowed to glide even before they can legally do all manner of other things. There are now about 5,000 flights a year. The highest flight went to an incredible 34,000ft, which is up where commercial aircraft fly, not that I'd ever want to spot one when I'm up there. Some things have changed down the years. When I last went gliding at Sutton Bank a little plane pulled me airborne, but previously the gliders were propelled into the air using a winch powered by a very posh car: a 1923 convertible Rolls Royce Silver Ghost, purchased for £50 in 1937. It was ideal because it was a heavy car and in excellent mechanical condition. Someone drove the vehicle to the launch point before it was jacked up to get it off the ground. A drum of wire was then attached to one of its rear wheels; the other end was hooked up to the glider. The Rolls was then put in gear and "driven" – of course going nowhere, but creating the necessary force to get a powerless glider off the ground. As club member and former chairman Graham Evison put it to me: "Health and safety would have a field day." I can't imagine government officials nowadays would have liked a horse being used either, but one was. He was called Major. His task for a while in the 1930s was to retrieve the flying machines and the winch wire. All went well until a glider hit the poor animal. From then on, Major galloped away when landings were imminent. He clearly wasn't daft.

Before he retired Graham, a horticulturalist, grew cucumbers for a living. He's been flying at the club since 1966 and now visits it twice a week. He obviously knows what he's doing by now and some of his flights last for hours. He was brimming with intriguing stories as we chatted in the club's café, upstairs on the first floor where the view is better. He showed me round the building, which is unusual because the main bit is circular. The 1960s architect apparently liked creating round structures, and I like this one. Big windows let in lots of light and offer impressive views of flights and the country-side. Graham gave me a wide-ranging history lesson about the site, explaining that it's surrounded by the defences of an Iron Age fort. He mixes history with odd facts, like telling me that the distance record for a glider from the club is 850 km, "from here to Cardiff Bay and back, via Cambridge."

On the walls of the clubhouse are a number of photographs, including, at the top of the stairs, a large black and white one of three men. "They were founding members, the Sharp brothers," said Graham. "They sold greeting cards and had a factory in Bradford. Eventually, they sold the business to Clinton cards, making them wealthy men. One of them, Norman, helped the club buy its first bit of land." Another brother, Donald, met his future wife Daphne at the club in the 1930s and quickly whisked her off to Thirsk's Golden Fleece pub for a date. She was worth millions when she died decades later and left the club some of her money. I think Graham knows how much, but he was far too polite to say.

Administrator Josephine Runciman, one of a handful of people employed by the gliding club, is another gold mine of information. After telling me she'd recently managed to persuade Graham to take a feral cat off her hands, she moved on to talk about early pilots being real adventurers: "They were the equivalent of today's Bear Grylls." She explained that glider maker Fred Slingsby would bring over what he had made during the week, "throw it off the edge and pick up the bits. He repaired it then brought it back." Tragically, there have been accidents over the years, including two fatal ones a decade or so ago. But as Josephine rightly pointed out, every sport has accidents. "I'd say 99% of them can be put down to human error. Gliding is actually incredibly safe."

Over the years the club has had some very wealthy benefactors. A Thai royal called Prince Bira – a grandson of King Mongkut, the inspiration for the monarch in the musical *The King And I* – was friendly with Fred Slingsby. Graham, Josephine and I ended up chatting about Bira after I spotted a bust of Fred sitting on an office shelf. It turned out the Asian aristocrat sculpted it, and Fred at some point built a glider for him.

Born in 1914 and educated at Eton, and later at art college, Bira was clearly a talented sculptor if the bust is anything to go by. He even exhibited at the Royal Academy in London. Unsurprisingly, my favourite part of the Bira story involves an animal. It's said the prince sometimes took a little white dog (possibly a Highland Terrier) called Titch gliding with him, perhaps even perched on his shoulders. I can't think of this duo without laughing, wondering if the dog wore goggles and what it did if it needed to pee, thousands of feet up. Bira clearly thrived on adrenaline rushes and packed an awful lot into his life; he was also a Formula One racing car driver (Asia's first), a sailor in four Olympic Games, and a pilot who taught RAF men how to fly in the Second World War. He must have decided life in the fast lane meant just that, whether on land, sea or in the air.

Fortunately, being a royal meant he didn't have to worry about money and the mundane, everyday matters we lesser mortals have to deal with. He was well connected, supping tea with prime ministers and sitting in the Royal Box at Ascot. When Bira landed in a farmer's field he'd simply call his chauffeur to organise a removal van to go and collect his glider, Graham told me.

Unfortunately, this remarkable life came to a rather abrupt end when Bira died from a heart attack at a London tube station in 1985. The police eventually identified him from a handwritten note in Thai, found in his pocket and addressed to Prince Bira. I have no idea what happened to Titch. But wouldn't it be nice to think he's still flying high with his master in a sunny afterlife, yapping excitedly at the sight of the white horse?

CHAPTER 6

The Road to Whitby

I had no set route in mind. I was just heading in the general direction of Whitby, and to get to that historic coastal town I would have to travel northeast across the Yorkshire Moors. Over recent decades people have spent small fortunes travelling the world to visit ever-more exotic locations, but sometimes the best places can be right on your doorstep. Sometimes these places are so close that we hardly notice they are there. I think the tide has turned a little and people are now beginning to appreciate their own backyards: the "staycation" has become fashionable, as holidaymakers decide to explore what's close at hand.

I've always been enchanted by the rugged Moors, so I decided to give myself a day off to recharge my batteries, I wanted to revisit some of the places I'd known all my life. I wanted somewhere both familiar and beautiful. What could be better than the road to Whitby?

I decided to head first towards the valley of Farndale, famous for its daffodils, so much so that it's known as the Daffodil Dale. When they are in bloom, Farndale is choc-a-bloc with visitors. I knew I wouldn't be seeing many flowers or tourists on this particular journey because it was still early in the year. In fact, spring had

The atmospheric and spooky Whitby Abbey, one of the gems of the Yorkshire coastline.

hardly got going. It was very chilly and I was heading higher up still, where it would be even chillier…I often visited Farndale and its meadows and woodlands with my family as a child. I'd travel squeezed in next to my Granny Duncalf in the back seat of the car; sometimes I'd be perched on her lap. Of course, those were the days before seat belts were compulsory, but luckily we didn't come to any harm. Usually we didn't have a walk (my mother wasn't a fan of walking for leisure) but we would take in the daffodils from the car window then stop for tea and scones in a village tearoom.

On one trip my father disappeared into a field for a call of nature and was gone for almost an hour. My mother's anxiety turned to fury when he returned and said he'd been chatting to an interesting farmer and had lost track of time. Now I was returning on my own. It wasn't just refreshing to put work behind me for a few hours – it would also be a trip down memory lane. Like many of us, I make these journeys all the time in my head, but it's also nice to do them for real once in a while. I'm beginning to realise I shouldn't keep putting things off. I'm not getting any younger.

I'd been reminded of that fact just before I set off when I'd been unusually distracted from my breakfast by the radio. My young colleague, vet Guy Killick, had been on air explaining how he'd used fish skin to save a dying spaniel called Gigha. She'd been suffering from a seriously infected wound on her elbow after cutting herself when she fell into a ditch. Guy had used the skin of a tilapia fish as a kind of biological bandage to help the wound heal. It helped the four-year-old dog's own skin regenerate. Gigha had completely recovered and was running around again, as giddy as ever. Guy was suddenly popular with journalists wanting to hear all about his inventive cure. A skin graft using tilapia fish skin had been used successfully on a horse with acid burns before, but the procedure had never been used to treat an infected wound, or used on a dog. I was delighted for Gigha and delighted for Guy, but was also feeling my age and a bit out of the loop. I'd never done an operation involving fish skin and knew I was unlikely to start now. It made me realise that there is another generation of vets coming up behind me and that my life as a vet would not go on forever. My decision to take a day off had been a good one. I needed to get out and enjoy myself.

I had no fixed idea which way I wanted to go, but I was enjoying driving past bustling hedgerows and pockets of snowdrops. On a whim, I decided to visit a tiny hamlet called Church Houses, which nestles between the dales of Farndale and Rosedale. I'd not been for years, but had spent a couple of happy weeks there on school trips when I was not only tall but gangly and spotty too. I wanted to see if the hostel my classmates and I had stayed in was still there.

I soon passed through Helmsley, the only market town in the Moors. I'd been there a couple of days before to treat a horse and that made me remember I needed a new ink pad for stamping horse passports, something a vet has to do after giving vaccinations. I'd gone to see a horse's lame leg. "She doesn't kick," the owner had said. She was wrong. The horse had lashed out and destroyed my ink pad, which was still in my hand, but luckily not me.

As I passed near the village of Pockley, I recalled a lovely old man called Oliver Dowkes, who'd lived in a smallholding with his dogs and Shire horses not far from there. He'd only recently died. It was yet another reminder, if I was looking for one, that life is short. I soaked up the scenery, feeling pleased I wasn't at work. These days I only spend about twenty percent of my working week outside the four walls of the practice, significantly less than I used to. So, there's always a spring in my step when I'm off on a farm job. As I drove through yet another village, Gillamoor, I saw a man walking along the street. He was stooping slightly, and wearing a woolly hat and wellies – a farmer. His life might still be hard, I thought, but probably not nearly as hard as the lives of his ancestors. They'd have had no central heating or other mod cons: no NHS either.

I enjoyed seeing the small buildings and sheds of typical Moors farms, made of a lovely pale stone. I slowed down for a woman on a horse and then for a van driver who was hurtling towards me. An advert on the side of his van said he had the uncommon job of inseminating cows with bull semen. Perhaps he'd been rushing to his next job!Before I knew it I was in Church Houses, where I immediately spotted and recognised the Feversham Arms pub. I drove around for a couple of minutes to get my bearings, passing some beautifully done up holiday cottages and a new brightly varnished wooden construction. "That needs to mellow," I said to myself. I found out later it was the new village hall. I finally pulled up at the solid-looking building I'd come to see. In my youth it had been a school, before being turned into a hostel for outdoor activities. I felt rather sad it was now a house, with blinds and plants in the windows.

"That room behind those windows must have been the kitchen," I thought. We'd all cooked, about 15 teenage lads, all peeling goodness knows how many potatoes for everything-can-go-in stews. The teachers often left us to it in the evenings, going for a drink in the Feversham Arms while we played cards or football, enjoying messing around without supervision. During the day we'd hike for hours through the Moors. We didn't think anything of walking 15 or 20 miles. We'd read our maps, eat huge mounds of sandwiches and laugh at our ridiculous, immature banter while enjoying the scenery and learning a bit about nature. I remember once we stuck out our thumbs and hitched a ride back to the hostel on the back of a big truck. We weren't tired, though. We just wanted to wind our teachers up. They arrived back an hour after we did, and it's fair to say we got a real rollicking!An hour later, back in the here and now, I was sipping a caffe latte in the picturesque village of Hutton-le-Hole. It's so named because it lies in a natural hollow – or 'hole'. It's as green as green can be, with sheep grazing by the stream that meanders through the village. Tourists, who flock there in their droves, regularly photograph them. A whole service industry has been set up to cater for them – the tourists, that is, not the sheep. Visitors can even buy diabetic chocolates, which are made in the village. I suppose diversification is the name of the game these days.

I'd driven to Hutton-le-Hole via Blakey Ridge, a remote and sometimes bleak spot. The 16th-century Lion Inn pub on top of the ridge was built at the highest point of the Moors. It's actually one of the highest pubs in England. As you can imagine, the views from there are beyond stunning. It serves good food too, no doubt much appreciated by the staff and visitors who were snowed in for nine days a few years ago. Although it wasn't snowing when I went to Blakey Ridge, the weather had turned nasty. It was windy and had begun to rain. I still pulled over to hop out for a quick walk, but realised I'd left my gloves and boots at home. Then I had a brainwave. I'd go to Hutton-le-Hole and knock on an old friend's door. At that moment I spotted a swooping sparrow hawk; I took it to be a good omen.

Of course, I was wrong about the good omen. I knew my friend Brian, a former pharmaceutical rep I'd not seen in years, had retired from selling medicines to run a tearoom in the village. But it was closed and then I discovered that not only was he not in, he'd moved away. A woman walking her two dogs in the rain told me Brian had been gone for ages. At least he wasn't dead, I told myself, but I was still disappointed. It would have been nice to reminisce. Reps would often visit our veterinary practice in Thirsk to try to sell their wares, and we became friends with many of them over cups of tea. Sometimes my old boss Donald would suddenly breeze in.

"Morning," he'd say sternly. "Any free samples today?"

"No, not today," the rep would murmur.

"Good day!" barked Donald before walking out, slamming the door behind him.

So, in need of caffeine and warmth, I popped into a café called The Forge, with a nice view across the long and winding village green. The Beatles' 'Love Me Do' was playing in the background while I ordered my coffee and began to put the world to rights with friendly owners Sarah and Peter, from Hull. They told me they'd left the city and their busy shift-work jobs a few years ago. The change had come about rather suddenly; they'd simply visited Hutton-le-Hole one day and fallen in love with it. But whereas most people would have done nothing to fuel the new love affair, this couple did. Within a week they'd handed in their notice at work. The café had just come on the market, so they snapped it up. They now get great reviews and have a delicious-sounding menu. I didn't partake as I was watching my waistline, but I can vouch for the coffee and service.

There are certainly plenty of local characters to keep them occupied. As we chatted, the door opened and in walked a comedian cunningly disguised as a postman called Dave. In his mid-60s, with glasses and a grey mini-quiff, Dave looks a bit like an ageing Elvis. Later, I heard three ladies refer to him with affection as the singing

Travelling back in time:
The Victorian Cottage
at the Ryedale Folk
Museum in beautiful
Hutton-le-Hole.

postman, and I wished I'd heard him croon. He's an unforgettable character. One of the first things he said to me was: "You might find this hard to believe, but I was an ugly baby. I was so ugly, a doctor slapped my mother." Followed by: "When I was a kid my uncle and auntie gave me pocket money. I was told to put it in my moneybox. I was 12 before I realised it was a gas meter." "Who is your scriptwriter?" I asked him with a groan, and a laugh. Dave has been a postman for about 20 years, but delivering the post is only part of who he is. He's one of those people who can put a smile on anyone's face and makes it his mission to do so. I bet it takes him a while to get through his shift, though.

After Dave had finally gone (he kept reappearing to crack more jokes) I walked to the village museum, the Ryedale Folk Museum. There's a lot to see, inside and out. I was having a whale of a time, but feeling strange. You know you're old when you see items from your own childhood in a museum, although some of the artefacts go back much further than the 1950s, to medieval and Elizabethan times. Some are from the Iron Age. I walked past a 100-year-old plough that looked like the one I have at home in the garage; I did it up decades ago.

Then I felt the irresistible pull of the museum's reconstructed old buildings, which included a blacksmith's workshop. I could almost visualise the blacksmith's run by Bill Armstrong in the village when I was a boy. I'd pop in to keep warm while I waited for the school bus to collect me. Blacksmiths shoed horses and made or repaired farm tools and implements used by other craftsmen. A museum sign explained that they were often skilled vets too, and occasionally treated humans, setting bones and concocting herbal remedies. Reading it, Bill went up in my estimation.

In the museum's tiny village shop, forever frozen in 1953, a little bell tinkled as I entered. I could almost feel my Granny Duncalf pressing coins into my little sweaty hand to buy some liquorice allsorts. There were old packets of Typhoo tea, and the Shredded Wheat and digestive biscuit packets of my youth. I was tickled pink to spot some medicated toilet paper, rather like tracing paper. I'd forgotten all about it. I'd used it at school like lots of children did, but it didn't do what it was designed to do very well. I winced at the memory, then chuckled when I saw some old cigarettes. Granny Wright's brother Richard smoked them – Player's Navy Cut – from the age of 14. He stopped buying them when he turned 70, as he said they had become too expensive. He decided to switch to Woodbines. Uncle Richard was one of the exceptions to the rule that smoking kills. He smoked heavily for seven decades and died an old man.

The museum also has an undertaker's building that houses a magnificent black Victorian hearse. I nearly jumped out of my skin because I remembered spotting something similar on my school trips to Church Houses, stored in a shed near the church. Museum staff told me later their hearse was that very vehicle. It had been bought second-hand by the people of Farndale in 1839. I also lingered over some old farming machines. There was one for slicing up fodder beet, grown for cattle, and another brilliant one invented to scoop potatoes out of the soil. There was also a threshing machine, which, in the time before combine harvesters, was used to remove corn from stalks and husks. I remembered standing in farmyards as a youngster, watching a tractor power a mobile threshing machine. They were big and cost a lot of money, so travelled from farm to farm. I'd help to fork sheaves of corn into the machine. It was also good fun to watch because as the corn was fed in, swarms of rats and mice would dash out as their hiding places were eaten up by the machine. Dogs would catch them or bystanders like me would kill them by hitting them with sticks. As a child it was very exciting.

CHAPTER 7

A Brief Encounter

got back in my car and decided to head to the town of Pickering at the foot of the Yorkshire Moors. Seeing the museum of bygone days at Hutton-le-Hole had given me an idea. I didn't want to just see the past. I wanted to actually experience it. In order to do that I needed to go to Pickering, ditch the car and take a different form of transport.

It didn't take me long to get there and, once I'd parked up, I made my way through a doorway and up a short flight of stone steps into a solid-looking, one-storey building. I stepped through and out onto a platform, where crowds of people were already gathered. I was at the southern terminus of the North Yorkshire Moors Railway, home to one of the finest steam journeys in the country. It used to be a working line, running between Pickering and Whitby. It carried cargo and people from 1836 until the infamous Dr Beeching decided in the 1960s that the line, along with many others across Britain, needed to go. Fortunately, local people decided to re-open the railway and run it as a celebration of steam. Now it's thriving, transporting tourists who want to experience the real romance of travel.

I and the other eager passengers didn't have long to wait. At first I noticed how people who'd crammed onto the bridge that spans the line were staring into the distance. Just at that moment we all heard what we'd come to hear – a magical chug, chug, chugging, and the hissing of brakes. I spun around to see a huge cloud of steam. The crowd was teased with more noise and smoke for a few more seconds then, suddenly, there it was, a huge dark green locomotive called *The Golden Arrow*. As it sailed into view, pulling about ten maroon-coloured carriages, I caught sight of three or four men in the cab, and momentarily envied them. Just for a second or two I was a schoolboy again, and for the first time in more than half a century I thought: I want to be a train driver when I grow up.

I quickly climbed up and onto the bridge for a different perspective, briefly distracted from the train as I peered down on a group of beautifully dressed ladies next to the locomotive. They were taking photographs of a woman in a white dress who could only have been a bride. I'd actually spotted the wedding party getting off a double-decker bus outside the station a few minutes before. The railway line is such a draw that even couples tying the knot want to include it in their big day.

Turning my head, I could see the modern world of Pickering beyond the station – but looking back at the steam train, it was easy to forget all that existed. The station itself added to the illusion. I caught sight of a reassuring red telephone box, an old WH Smith kiosk, and historic adverts for Weetabix and Brooke Bond tea. There were even three gleaming red fire buckets. I'd gone back in time, and I was loving it.

As I ambled back onto the platform, I noticed a few more nicely turned out people, clearly invited to the nuptials. Some carriages had tables that had been covered with whiter-than-white table-cloths. On top, there were fancy little cakes on stands, just waiting to be eaten. A white-haired guard wearing a peaked cap leaned out of a door and told me the train was bound for Grosmont, a village in the heart of the North York Moors. He said the cakes were for the bridal party, which was being served afternoon tea on board. "It's their wedding reception," he said with a smile. I smiled back. Weddings, and their promise of good times ahead, tend to cheer everyone up. After a few minutes, the engine suddenly came to life and, with its bridal party safely on board, *The Golden Arrow* slid out of view.

My train would be heading along the same track a few minutes later, so I went to buy a ticket. The ticket seller was a jovial chap with a colourful patterned waistcoat. A proper sight for sore eyes.

"You look smart in that waistcoat," I said.

"It used to be a carpet," he joked. At least, I think he was joking.

With a few minutes to spare, I had a peep in the station shop. It was full of people and too many items I had no desire to buy, so I walked out and into the quaint and busy tearoom instead. An excellent decision, even if there was no time to sit down for a cup of tea. It has a lovely old-fashioned look, with wooden floors, a fireplace and, perhaps unsurprisingly, lots of paintings of trains. I even glimpsed a young couple in matching tweed jackets holding hands across a table, the woman's hair pulled up in a chignon. It could almost have been 1943, with the chap home on leave from the War, poised to ask his sweetheart to marry him. I realised my imagination was running away with me. I had a train to catch.

We were a few minutes late leaving Pickering, but that didn't matter. All the more time to sit on board a carriage pulled by a big green locomotive called *Repton*. They're made of stern stuff, these engines, and they have to be: this railway line has some of the steepest gradients of any line in Britain. Fen Bog, the highest point, is 150 metres above sea level. As I flicked through my guidebook, aptly entitled *Relive the Glory of Steam*, I stared out of the window and chatted to a couple of other passengers, feeling like a kid in a sweet shop. At Skeldale that week, our brilliant head nurse Rachel had handed in her notice. It was a real blow to me (luckily she changed her mind later), but the train and its soothing sound were already proving to be a welcome diversion.

We'd barely pulled out of the station when Gill Brown, in charge of the dining part of the train, popped up with a question. I heard later she'd been a regular extra in the TV series *Heartbeat*, filmed for years in and around Goathland, the railway's most popular stop. She wanted to know if I'd pop down the train to see a lady celebrating her birthday. "It's her 60th and she's a big fan of *The Yorkshire Vet*," Gill said. I set off, passing through several carriages of people and a few quiet dogs. I was a little unsteady on my feet as the train twisted and turned on its way through the North York Moors National Park. I almost stumbled past a couple of waiters carrying trays of desserts on sparkling crockery before I arrived at Liz from York's birthday bash. One of her friends said I'd have really made her day if I'd had Jeanie Green from *The Yorkshire Vet* with me. I hope Liz thought I was better than nothing.

On my way back to my seat a young volunteer caught my eye. He was wearing a smart black uniform with a number of badges pinned to it. His name was Nathan Walker and he was just 20. As we chatted he pointed to one of his favourite badges: it was a tiny image of the *Mallard*, the fastest steam locomotive ever built.

Nathan is one of the hundreds of volunteers who ensure this short railway line keeps running. At 16 he became a volunteer ticket inspector, before being promoted to his current position: a guard. He told me that he'd been fascinated by trains since he was four years old. "It all started with *Thomas the Tank Engine*," he grinned. Good old Thomas. I'd also enjoyed the books about him and his friends as a child. They partly explain why my brother and I had been so keen to watch trains go by on the East Coast line not far from our home. If the drivers tooted, they made our day. Nathan, in contrast, was right in the thick of it, every Saturday. How lucky was he, I thought. And how nice of him to give up so much of his free time.

We were making sedate progress along the line, travelling as far as I could make out at about 25mph. But the *Repton* engine pulling us could, in its time, get up to 100mph. "It was the racehorse of its day," said a man sitting nearby who seemed to be a fount of knowledge when it came to steam trains. "When it finished with British Rail it was taken to America, and pulled trains there before a Norwegian guy brought it here about 20 years ago," he told me. The man's name was Kieran Murray. He is one of dozens of people who are actually employed by the line. He's the carriage and wagon manager, which means he's in charge of all restoration. He's a self-confessed machine fanatic who would have loved to have been around in the age of steam. I actually met him on his day off, but something had needed fixing, so he'd been called out. Although he's only in his early 30s, he's been a North York Moors Railway fixture for more than half his life. "I came here as a naughty boy from school," Kieran laughed. What he meant was that his first contact with the steam railway began with a work placement when he was a 14-year-old, living on his family's farm. From that moment on he's had the railway bug.

His story reminded me of how I fell into veterinary medicine. When I was a teenager, unsure what to do for a career, a teacher suggested I might enjoy being a vet. He knew the vets Alf and Jim Wight, so arranged for me to do work experience with them. Like me, Kieran was fortunate to stumble across his calling. He has learned how to drive trains as well as fix them, and even mends them in his spare time. He recently finished restoring a First World War railway handcar that was used near the trenches.

As we tootled along at a steady pace, Kieran told me he'd also been on television, in Channel 5's *Yorkshire Steam Railway* series. He was even filmed in Sri Lanka. But that's not his only claim to fame: he now lives in Goathland's station house. Both the station and village are familiar to millions of people who haven't even been to Britain, let alone to Yorkshire. That's because ITV's *Heartbeat* series, the first *Harry Potter* film and BBC1's *All Creatures Great and Small*, based on the Herriot books, are just some of the programmes that have used it for location filming. Kieran appeared as an extra in *Harry Potter and the Philosopher's Stone* and met Harry himself, in the form of actor Daniel Radcliffe. Harry Potter fans and other tourists show up at Kieran's home. "I occasionally find an American in my house," he laughed.

With all this chatting, I realised I was missing the scenery, so extracted myself from Kieran and went to sit down, saying hello to some *Yorkshire Vet* fans from Reading on my way. "Reading? The Deep South," I joked. "Doncaster is far enough south for me."

Back in my seat, I looked out of the window and read a little about the financial cutbacks made to the train network following Dr Beeching's recommendations in the 1960s. Luckily, the North Yorkshire Moors Railway Preservation Society was set up to save

Luggage and trolleys from a bygone age at Pickering station, the terminus of the North Yorkshire Moors Railway.

PICKERING

this particular line. The first volunteers believed that trips along 24 miles of one of the most historic railway lines in Britain, surrounded by gorgeous scenery and near a beautiful coastline, had plenty of tourist potential. Now the railway is so popular it struggles to meet demand: there are more than 300,000 visitors a year. The society has about 10,000 paying members; there are 550 volunteers, 100 full-time staff and 50 seasonal workers. An impressive list. Some volunteers even travel from overseas, like two young women from Wisconsin in the United States who wanted to learn how to drive a steam train. Some volunteers stay for months at a time.

The charity that runs the railway had a fantastic financial boost not long ago, receiving millions of pounds of lottery money, some of it for sheds to protect carriages from the elements. All the cash and manpower is needed, as it's expensive and time-consuming to maintain this wonderful piece of history. When the railway is closed to tourists during the winter, there's still a long list of things to do. Even the youngest locomotive is more than 50 years old; overhauling just that one engine costs around half a million pounds. Maintenance staff are always busy. When the repairs have been done there are countless hours of varnishing and painting to do, which is, I imagine, rather like painting the Forth Bridge: it never ends. One man paints carriages entirely by hand. He must be the most patient man in Yorkshire.

We were now well into the Moors and, although I saw several yellow, spiky gorse bushes, I couldn't see any purple heather; it would be out later on in the year. The Moors are an internationally important heather moorland, maintained by grazing and inter-mittent burning or cutting of the heather for grouse, small birds bred to be shot. If this management of the land didn't happen, the area would be covered with scrub woodland. We'd already passed through Levisham, with its old-fashioned iron lamppost and cute station house complete with pretty garden. A man and a little lad didn't see me watching them step happily out of the house and onto the platform in their socks to look at the train, just as dads and their sons have done for generations.

I was at this point having a lovely conversation with David and Rachel, a Northallerton couple sitting just across the aisle. Their friends were clients of mine: small world. Their little boy Cameron liked tractors, so we compared notes when we stopped briefly in Goathland. I didn't have time to get off for a wander around (a shame, as I knew of some beautiful walks from the village), but Cameron made up for that. Munching on a ham sandwich, he told me about the nursery he attends which has what can only be described as a farm attached to it, to give children the chance to see something of the outdoors. Cameron told me he often helps to collect eggs, and enjoys seeing the lambs and chickens. Before I knew it, the train was off again and before long pulling into Grosmont, where I said goodbye to my new friends as Cameron headed off with his parents to see the station's cats.

I got off the train too to stretch my legs, which allowed me a good look at the steaming, hissing beast I'd be transported on. It really is a marvel that in the age of electric railways there's still something like this to offer a glimpse of the past. Later on, I got a chance to look round one of the massive workshops at Pickering. I scrambled around some old carriages that are being restored to their former glory. One of them dated back to 1894. Many of the volunteers who do the restoration work were employed by the railways before they retired. One was a fascinating chap called Eddie Knorn who told me he'd once had a railway carriage in his back garden for a while. "It filled most of it. I wanted it to be my shed," he said. Sadly for him – but perhaps not his neighbours – the council said no and the carriage was removed.

Pickering's restorers work on every nut and bolt the public don't see, as well as everything on board. In one carriage where a small bar was being installed, I noticed a plaque for a local lady called Betty. She died a couple of years ago in her late 80s and left thousands of pounds to the railway to be spent on restoration. It's money like this that allows the work to continue.

But such generosity is sometimes countered by less worthy acts. I was shocked to discover, while standing in a wooden carriage from the 1930s well on its way to being in tip-top condition, that it was one of seven broken into by a group of teenagers a couple of years ago. They went on the rampage and caused thousands of pounds' worth of damage, some of it to irreplaceable items. One of the vandalised carriages had taken volunteers years to restore. Mirrors were broken, and light fittings and wooden panels smashed. Stolen food and wine were consumed by the vandals and thrown around to make even more of a mess. Kieran, the restoration manager, said he'd received a phone call when the discovery was made. "It was like a war zone," he said.

I felt angry, unable to understand the mentality of these idiots, but was pleased to hear Kieran describe how the community had come together after the incident. "Shopkeepers and other people came to help us put everything back together again. There was loads of local support and donations. There were more people wanting to help than I could manage." The culprits who wreaked havoc were found and fined peanuts. But at least they had the decency to plead guilty.

Back at Grosmont, the whistle blew and the train departed for its final stop: Whitby, that little jewel of a town on the edge of the North Sea. For much of its existence Whitby, with the bleak and inaccessible Moors to its back and the raging ocean to the front, was isolated from the rest of the country. In fact, for many years the water was the best way in and out, and Whitby was a town of whaling and shipbuilding.

As the centuries moved on, both those industries went into decline, but trains helped restore a little pride to Whitby. The Pickering steam railway now used by day-trippers and history buffs was originally built to help keep the town's economy alive. For a good many years it worked. The track linked Whitby to the rest of the country, and new industries developed along the line: there were stone quarries, lime kilns and the beginnings of a tourist industry. These days trains and roads bring in goodness knows how many visitors, and there's plenty for them to see. The water's not as warm as the English Channel, not to mention the Mediterranean, but the fishing port's ancient abbey, quirky old streets and award-winning beaches make up for that. And who could visit and not have a generous portion of fish and chips, some of the finest in England?

The town is also renowned for its fossils from the Jurassic period. These are constantly being unearthed by the never-ending erosion of soft, clay cliffs by the action of the sea. Whitby has even developed something of a reputation for horror – and you can see why. As you look down on the town from the height of the rain-swept moors, it takes on an eerie aspect. That's probably why Bram Stoker, who visited many times, decided to set part of his novel, *Dracula*, in Whitby. Anyone standing on the cliff top next to the ruined abbey at night might expect the icy touch of a vampire.

Captain James Cook, the explorer who charted the coastlines of New Zealand and Australia, lived and worked in Whitby for a while, too. He was born nearby, and two of the ships he sailed in were built there. As much as I admire him, I wouldn't have wanted to travel in or out of this busy harbour in a sailing ship in the 1700s. Too adventurous for my liking: Pickering steam railway provided more than enough thrills for me.

CHAPTER 8

Saving Yorkshire

t was horrifying to see the open suitcase in front of me stuffed full of critically endangered tortoises and wrapped up in cling film so they couldn't move. It made me furious. These Ploughshare tortoises are the most threatened on the planet, largely because of illegal poaching. Despite the cost to the world's biodiversity, some sad individuals still want to own them as pets. It's even more astonishing when you realise that these tortoises are only found in the wild in north-western Madagascar. Recent research is grim reading, to say the least. It suggests there might not be any left in the wild at all.

Fortunately for the animals – and for my blood pressure – the precious contents of the luggage were not real. They were part of a mock-up of what had been found at Bangkok airport in 2013. The Thai authorities had discovered 54 of these beautiful, golden-domed tortoises in a single bag. A lot of them were still tiny. They'd been barely able to move because of their plastic wrapping, but many were apparently still alive. The smugglers don't want them to die. They can make a lot of money selling them as illegal, high-status, trophy pets to wealthy people who seem to act like they're buying a fancy car or a designer outfit.

21 critically endangered Radiated tortoises were found along with the Ploughshares, and a 38-year-old Thai man was arrested trying to collect what was probably a rather heavy bag at a luggage carousel. It turned out he hadn't even been a passenger on a flight; he must have had help gaining access to the restricted area. Amazingly, he'd been arrested a few weeks previously for smuggling. The suitcase had been registered to a 25-year-old woman from Madagascar, who'd flown in that day. She was also arrested. Ironically, a conference on the global wildlife trade had only just ended in Thailand. The discovery of the tortoises made it clear there was still a huge amount of work to be done. Just hours before the Ploughshares were found, airport officials also came across 300 Indian Star tortoises and ten Black Pond turtles, which are also endangered, in an unclaimed bag. The courier must have chickened out, too scared to go through security and run the risk of getting caught.

The mock-up of the suitcase found at Bangkok airport was on display at Jersey Zoo. If you're wondering about the connection between those two places, I'll explain. The aim of the zoo is not just to give people the opportunity to see wild animals up close, but also to teach the public about conservation. I was there not long ago to do some filming for a Channel 5 TV programme called *Big Week at the Zoo*. The film crew and I headed to Jersey in the Channel Islands because the head vet at the zoo is my old university friend and housemate, Andy Routh. "It's all so depressing," I complained as I looked at the suitcase. "It really does show what harm man can do to our beloved animals." Andy told me that the Ploughshare tortoises found in Bangkok had probably managed to stay alive on the long flight there because their heads had not been as restricted as their limbs, allowing them to breathe. He said they'd also survived because they are cold-blooded animals and their metabolisms slow down when it gets a bit chilly – which it certainly must have been 30,000ft up, in the hold of an aircraft.

Andy has built up a vast wealth of knowledge, and not just about the rare Ploughshare tortoise, which gets its name from a bony extension that juts out from the underside of its shell and looks like the cutting edge of a plough.

I first met this fellow Yorkshireman (he's from Leeds) when we were both studying veterinary medicine in Liverpool in the 1970s. After qualifying, Andy worked as a regular vet while volunteering in the wildlife sector. He eventually landed his first paid job in the field and went on to work around the world, in places such as Hong Kong, Indonesia and the United States. Now he's head vet for the Durrell Wildlife Conservation Trust, which is based at Jersey Zoo. It's a fabulous place that has a particular focus on endangered species. Although I didn't enjoy much of what I learned from one of my oldest mates (it was frankly depressing to hear a lot of it), I was pleased to see him and pleased to be there.

The zoo has 32 acres of lush landscaped gardens and thousands of animals, from gorillas and orang-utans to St Lucia parrots and Komodo dragons. It was summertime when I was there and there were flowers in abundance. Although I'm sometimes reluctant to leave Yorkshire, I would happily make a regular trip to Jersey. Its zoo was set up in 1959 by naturalist and author Gerald Durrell who wrote, among other books, *My Family And Other Animals*, which has been filmed several times for both the large and small screen.

As I followed Andy into a reptile house, I hesitated at a red sign stating: "Staff only. Trespassers will be swallowed!"

"Is it safe?" I asked my friend.

"You're too big to be swallowed," he laughed.

Once inside, we kneeled down to look at a Ploughshare tortoise. This time I was looking at a real one that was about 40cm long and weighed about 8kg. As the cute little fella munched away on his green lunch, Andy told me that each tortoise is worth thousands of pounds to a poacher. Big ones can be sold for as much as £40,000 and, as my friend put it, they are easy to poach: you can just pick them up. Even if they are discovered while being trafficked, the chances of them surviving are slim. "Their immune system can be affected by exposure to a long period of cold," explained Andy.

After being rescued from poachers, many tortoises go on to develop diseases they cannot fight off. "As far as I know, none were known to be alive within a year or two of confiscation," Andy told me, referring to the Ploughshares found in Thailand. Poaching them also puts the survival of the entire species at risk, even if they don't die during or after transit. As Andy said: "Having gone through probably one illegal holding centre and then a Thai centre where confiscated tortoises, turtles and the like from all over Asia are held, they would have had no role in our conservation breeding programme because they would have been in contact with unfamiliar viruses, which can have a devastating impact."

I suddenly understood why the Durrell Trust moves heaven and earth to prevent tortoises from being stolen in the first place. The Trust actually has a breeding facility in Madagascar, home to what it calls an "indispensable safety net population". There, more than 600 tortoises have been born and 100 released into the wild. In 2011 the team were over the moon to discover some of the tortoises they had released were successfully breeding. But even the breeding facility has been targeted by poachers. It's a never-ending battle

The Nicholsons of Cannon Hall Farm with their prize winning Highland cow at The Great Yorkshire Show.

Opposite top: A stunning technicolour sunset over Lake Gormire. Opposite bottom: Gliders being towed into the wide open Yorkshire skies. They have been launched from Sutton Bank since the dawn of aviation.

This page top: Catching up on the latest news with Jim Wight, Alf Wight's son. We often bring his dog Cleo along for a stroll. This page bottom: One of Yorkshire Gliding Club's most illustrious members was Fred Slingsby, a First World war airman who won the Military Medal. Seen here far right.

This page:
Kilburn woodcarver,
Robert Thompson
"Mouseman" motif on
wooden furniture.
Opposite top and
bottom, views from
The North York
Moors National Park.
The famous White
Horse above Kilburn,
and black sheep on
heather-covered
moors.

Clockwise from top: The Boar's Head Hotel, Ripley, whose beer pumps were blessed by an obliging priest; Rosedale, an idyllic valley nestled in the heart of the North York Moors; The awesome power of Repton on the North Yorkshire Moors Railway; Whitby's 199 Steps leading to St. Mary's Church.

Local Heroes, clockwise from top: At the Great Yorkshire Show with Summer Ali, who wrote a wonderful poem about me, alongside her dad Paul and his partner Sadie; Caroline Howard, Manager of Askham Bryan Wildlife and Conservation Park; Emma Hornshaw, one of the many volunteers who work tirelessly looking after the Exmoor ponies at Askham Bog; Will Greensit and Chris Greensit (right), who discovered a cache of 17th-century gold coins on their farm.

to improve security with a limited pot of money. One method of discouraging theft has been to introduce an engraving system, which reduces the tortoises' market value for potential poachers. Engraving the shell of a tortoise is painless and means it can be easily identified by researchers and enforcement agencies. There's also another system to help the Ploughshares survive. It involves a transmitter being glued onto their shells. If a tortoise makes a sudden movement (obviously something they don't do on their own) an alarm is set off. A simple but clever idea.

Andy is in his element in Jersey, but was a bit of an oddity at university as he was fanatical about zoo work. "There weren't many people back then interested in zoos and conservation," he said. It's now clear he was ahead of the pack, but at the time he was out of step with his peers. Most of our classmates were, like me, interested in working with farm animals and pets. These days Andy is very much at the centre of things. His work is vital and increasingly fashionable but, unlike some fashions, conservation is one I'm glad to see taking off.

I'm also involved in the sector, as an ambassador for The Donkey Sanctuary. It's an international organisation transforming the lives of millions of donkeys and mules and the people who depend on them for their livelihoods. But there are easier and more everyday ways to help animals and the environment. The more people step up – from making a hedgehog box and hanging up a bird feeder to avoiding palm oil and eating sustainably sourced meat – the better off our fellow creatures will be.

When we'd seen the Ploughshares, Andy and I sat down for a few minutes and had a cup of tea and a chat next to a bed of beautiful flowers. We toasted our friendship and reflected on where we'd got to in life. "In the twilight of our careers, we've both probably ended up where we wanted to be," he said. I agreed, thinking that just as Alf Wight was a big influence on my life, Gerald Durrell had a big impact on Andy, even if they never met: Gerald died in 1995, years before Andy arrived in Jersey. Now it's up to Andy and me, and everyone else who cares about animals and the natural world, to continue the Herriot and Durrell legacies and pass the baton on.

Channel 5's *Big Week at the Zoo* was a documentary series celebrating some of the best conservation work carried out by British zoos. The series was based mostly at Yorkshire Wildlife Park near Doncaster, with my little bit with Andy and the tortoises, shot in Jersey.

On the programme I also discussed hedgehogs with presenters Helen Skelton and Nick Baker. It's blindingly obvious that it's not just the likes of Madagascan tortoises and Arctic polar bears that need our help. The hedgehog is increasingly rare in Britain, but if you are lucky enough to see one snuffling around in your garden, be careful with them, as I told the programme. They are lactose intolerant so they shouldn't be given milk. It can kill them. Puppy food and water is best.

The hedgehog is one of many animals in our own backyard that are in danger of disappearing for good. In fact, some species are so rare nowadays that they are on the way to seeming as exotic to us as the African lion. There are some frightening statistics relating to British wildlife. Between 1970 and 2013, 56 percent of species in the UK declined, according to the World Wildlife Fund. There have been some environmental successes of late: a few mammals, including otters, stoats and weasels, have been making a comeback in Britain, primarily because harmful human activities that were endangering them have stopped or been reduced. But, overall, we haven't looked after the world around us very well.

Some problems are the result of intensive farming. It's led to the loss of countless flower meadows, hedges and trees, all vital homes for pollinating insects such as bees. This often has a knock-on effect for other species in the food chain. Many of our iconic mammals, including moles and hedgehogs, eat invertebrates that like wetter weather, meaning they could all be threatened by climate change. A few months ago, a major report said Britain would miss almost all its 2020 nature targets that we signed up to a decade ago. We have failed to look after threatened species or end the degradation of our land. We've not ended unsustainable fishing or raised public awareness enough about the importance of biodiversity. Now we are facing the irreversible loss of plant and animal species and habitats, as well as dealing with the impact of climate change. It's all about having a balance in nature. We've lost that balance, and that needs to be addressed.

Thank goodness for Sir David Attenborough, one of the best-known advocates of the natural world. He's worked so hard for so long to show us what we might lose if we don't act to change our ways soon. Sir David is famous for travelling the world to make his documentaries, but he's also involved in conservation here in Britain. He is the "President Emeritus" of Britain's wildlife trusts and has even helped raise the profile of a tiny wildlife area in North Yorkshire. It shows the measure of the man that he can be bothered about something like Askham Bog, which most people simply flash past when driving along a busy road near York. I imagine most don't even know it's there.

The 43-hectare site has attracted naturalists from around the world for 200 years, and is one of the Yorkshire Wildlife Trust's key reserves. It's beautiful, and has also been designated a site of special scientific interest. Despite all that, the bog was recently threatened by proposals to build hundreds of houses on a next-door plot of land. Sir David was one of many people to criticise the plans. "If someone was proposing to put a building site next to York Minster, there would be an outcry," he said. "For naturalists, that's what this site is like. This is a treasure that is irreplaceable."

It's actually amazing the area has survived so long. It is only 66 metres from the A64 dual carriageway and a park-and-ride scheme is less than 40 metres away. But Askham Bog is still enchanting; wandering through, you can feel a world away from civilisation just round the corner. It feels as if time stands still. The bog has been described as a survivor of Yorkshire's ancient fenlands: a mosaic of fen, woodland and meadow on the site of an ancient lake left behind thousands of years ago by a retreating glacier. It oozes serenity.

The area was first officially recognised as important by the Society for the Promotion of Nature Reserves, set up by banker and expert naturalist Charles Rothschild in 1912. In May that year, just a few weeks after the *Titanic* sank, he held a meeting in London's Natural History Museum to talk about forming a new organisation to save Britain's best natural places. That get-together, in which he gathered naturalists from across the country to identify the best places to protect, led to the formation of the society. York's Askham Bog was named a key site and in 1946 was bought by York's famous sweet-makers Francis Terry and Arnold Rowntree. The Yorkshire Naturalists' Trust, now the Yorkshire Wildlife Trust, was created specifically in order to protect the bog.

The trust now looks after more than 100 nature reserves and has thousands of members and volunteers. But Askham Bog is extra special. It has a whole host of plant species, as well as creatures such as butterflies, frogs and birds. It's also a regular haunt for foxes, deer, water voles and ponies.

It has been carefully managed for more than seven decades to ensure it remains a haven for wildlife. I know Britain has a housing crisis, but looking around, there are plenty of brownfield sites to build on without having to threaten something as precious as the bog. It's crystal clear to many of us that concreting over more green spaces is not the answer.

There are, of course, many people other than Sir David trying to protect natural places like Askham Bog, and much of their work goes unnoticed and unmentioned. Veterinary student Emma Hornshaw, 19, is one. She has visited the bog countless times with her parents in the last few years. They regularly make the trip from their home in Tadcaster for a very special task: they are part of a volunteer team of pony checkers that keep an eye on the small herd of Exmoor ponies who live on the site from April to November. There's a maximum of six ponies grazing there at any one time, doing their own bit for the management of the bog. The Hornshaws have got to know many of the animals and handed over a great many carrots as treats. I know they mean well, but, as Emma will find out at university, too many carrots are not good for a pony's health.

Emma always wanted to be a vet, but needed more practical experience before her A levels and university applications. So she milked cows, helped with lambing, and did work experience with vets and the RSPCA. She even spent three days as a zookeeper. But it was the bog visits that became a family affair. The Hornshaws would look out for cuts on the ponies and ensure there was nothing in their eyes. They'd see if they were walking and eating properly and interacting.

"If a pony was on its own we reported back, because it could mean that it was being bullied and had become isolated," Emma said. Professional help was occasionally needed. "One pony had a hoof abscess so we called the emergency vet. Another one had a hip problem." Emma increased her usual twice-monthly volunteering to weekly when she began doing the Duke of Edinburgh award scheme. She recently received her gold award at Buckingham Palace.

All around Yorkshire there are volunteers trying to improve our environment and pass on their love of nature to the next generation. Emma Dawber, a former doctor in her mid-50s, has enjoyed volunteering at Flamborough on the East Coast so much that she's started doing a university degree in wildlife and conservation. She was a GP for more than 20 years and specialised in end-of-life care. For a few years now she's been a volunteer for the Yorkshire Wildlife Trust, inspiring people, especially school-children, to enjoy and understand the beach and the sea. She often takes youngsters rock pooling (some have never been to the beach before), pointing out creatures such as limpets and crabs. Sometimes she shows visitors seals bobbing around in the water or perched on nearby rocks. She also takes groups onto the beach to show them what they can find. Some items they pick up while beachcombing are turned into art. It's amazing what beautiful objects can be made from natural things, such as bones and dead crabs. But Emma also points out the destruction that can be inflicted on the natural environment by other pieces of flotsam and jetsam, such as plastic. Small, microscopic pieces of plastic are swallowed by fish and so get into the food chain. Bigger bits are dangerous too: birds often get tangled up in the detritus thrown overboard.

Emma still considers herself involved in health, albeit in a less formal way. She believes that being exposed to the great outdoors could be of more benefit to people than antidepressants. "If people have a healthy attitude to Mother Nature and to life, and are active doing something that makes them feel good, that's better than drugs," she said. I couldn't agree more. One of Emma's favourite tasks is taking summer visitors to see the colonies of puffins that gather on the sheer cliffs of Yorkshire's coastline. "It's amazing to show these wonderful birds to people who have never seen them before, and to people who are not usually into birds. Sometimes visitors squeal with delight," she said. The power our fellow creatures hold over us should never be underestimated.

Yorkshire Wildlife Park, where I filmed *Big Week at the Zoo*, is another example of how conservation is rapidly becoming more important. Hundreds of thousands of visitors pass through the 10-year-old park's doors each year, and it has done some excellent work on its 100 or so acres. It's been involved in international breeding and research programmes, and has England's only polar bears. In 2013 the park set up a conservation and welfare foundation that has raised more than £300,000. Lemurs, critically endangered black rhinos and lions are among the park's beneficiaries, but loved-up humans are too: they can get married on the site. No doubt there are some interesting wedding photographs. The Park is about more than animals though; it's even supported a major study that discovered a range of trees resistant to climate change.

Important work is being done near York on a smaller scale. There, the two-year-old Askham Bryan Wildlife and Conservation

Park is punching above its weight on a 17-acre site. It doesn't put on glamorous shows like Yorkshire Wildlife Park's *Wildest Wizard of Oz* performance involving professional actors, storytelling and wild animals; at Askham, not far from the bog I mentioned earlier, learning about animals and nature is more low-key. The park, open at weekends and in the school holidays, is home to creatures from all around the world. There are squirrel-sized monkeys, a gang of armadillos and chinchillas, meerkats, wallabies, and even a bird-eating spider. There's a lovely café too, which recently had an interesting display: a huge octopus mural made from bottle tops. And if you're lucky enough to see part-time education and retail assistant Jake English handle the reptiles, you are in for a treat. You can occasionally stroke them while hearing him share a whole host of gripping facts.

I know a bit about snakes, but not half as much as young Jake. He explained to one enthralled little girl recently that some snakes have special heat sensors just above their upper lip, which can detect body heat of prey like mice and rats. "Don't handle snakes when they've just been fed," he warned, the youngster hanging on his every word. "They sometimes throw up their food in order to become lighter, which enables them to escape faster. Snake vomit is projectile!"

Jake said he could easily pick out individuals among the park's numerous bearded dragons, which I have to say, all look alike to me. Then he was off on a fascinating tangent about lizards featuring in military research: scientists have been developing a material that could help humans climb a glass wall, inspired by the sticky toes of geckos. Other lizards can, amazingly, run on water for a short distance, Jake continued. He is, I think, perfect for his job. It was a little draining trying to keep up with him, but the children lapped it all up, their questions answered with aplomb.

The Conservation Park near York is actually part of Askham Bryan College, a well-known institution with several campuses in the north. It's been around for decades and runs a lot of courses, with a particular focus on agriculture and land management. It also prepares students for careers with animals. They might become veterinary nurses, animal keepers, research assistants or conservationists.

The mission is to inspire and educate future generations to respect and look after animals and plants. Caroline Howard, who's in her early 30s, has been the conservation park's boss since it opened in 2017. More than 50,000 people have visited already and there've been some early conservation successes, notably with the tansy beetle. There's a successful breeding patch on site, which is great news because the beetle, with its coppery sheen, is endangered. Some say the tiny creature was so admired by the Victorians that parts of its wings were used as sequins. I don't know if that's true, but looking at them I can almost believe it. The problem for the beetles is this: they only eat tansy plants, which are also in decline. If a clump disappears, the creatures have to make a difficult, often fatal, walk to a new clump, as they are not known to fly. That's why the appearance of new beetles is so cheering.

At just 16, Caroline became a weekend zookeeper, eventually becoming assistant manager after finishing her English Literature degree. She once had a scare with a lynx, which threw itself against the cage door just as she was closing it. Luckily she lived to tell the tale, and now she seems to know everything about every living thing. Bullets have been known to ricochet off the backs of armadillos, she said, and even caiman, bees, sharks and oysters can be trained. Chinchillas have the thickest fur of any land animal and were almost hunted to extinction. Skunk spray is like a garlicky, musky toilet with a grassy undertone. And orang-utans are "the best parents" because they keep their offspring around for up to a decade and suckle them for years. It's amazing how much she knows.

She loves all animals, big and small. "I get just as excited about a beetle as a tiger," she said. "Actually, I get a lot more excited about beetles. Did you know that nearly one in four of all known animal species is a beetle? They rule the world." Caroline has some interesting friends, too. One extracts venom from snakes so it can be used to make medicine for humans.

What all these people have in common is a love of the natural world and the knowledge that if we don't protect nature it won't be there for us. "It will cost us dearly as a species," said Caroline. "I want my daughter to grow up in a world full of the wonders of nature; I want her to see aye-ayes, and binturong, and Lord Howe Island stick insects, and partula snails." (I agree, even if I didn't know what some of those things were until I Googled them. Aye-ayes are endangered mammals in Madagascar, while binturongs are bearcats in Southeast Asia). Caroline continued: "But I also want her to live in a world that can enjoy the benefits of nature – the food, the nutrient cycling, the clean air, the compounds in nature that turn out to have medical value. How terrible would it be if the rosy periwinkle plant had become extinct before anyone discovered its use in treating cancer?" She's right, of course. I have a lot of experience with many medicines, including the common Foxglove, also known as *Digitalis purpurea*. Vets and doctors have used it for decades to treat congestive heart failure.

I sometimes wonder what Alf and Donald might have made of all this talk about conservation, because we had less information in their day about the damage we are causing the natural world. They didn't really have to think about protecting it. But they certainly loved nature. Alf's love of it was particularly clear to anyone who saw his contented face when he was walking in the countryside. His love was also obvious in his writing: he often described North Yorkshire's beauty in great detail. A 1982 *Reader's Digest* "best of" James Herriot book even had an additional seven-page colour section, with information about "nature in Herriot country". It mentioned various plants, birds and animals and was a celebration of them and their habitats, although the first few words were depressing. "Woods once covered North Yorkshire, but man and his animals have cleared most of them."

In Thirsk Museum I recently saw a couple of documents – a press release and a letter – from the late 1980s which made me remember how much Donald was also interested in the natural world and conservation. Both items were from the Nature Conservancy Council, a government agency dealing with, as the name suggests, conservation. The letter mentioned a visit one summer to Donald and his wife's huge 17th-century home, which stood on around 70 acres. The visit was part of a botanical survey of the North York Moors National Park. Apparently, the aim was to produce a map of the park's vegetation, but the success of the project was dependent on, as the agency put it, "the co-operation of landowners". There must have been some co-operation, because the council discovered many "additional species" such as *Athyrium filix-femina* (lady fern) and *Chamerion angustifolium* (rosebay willowherb). The letter was a rather dull read, but I was glad to see Donald had been interested enough to get involved. And there was one section that made me laugh out loud. It read: "I was very pleased to have been greeted with enthusiasm and was sorry that when I called back later to discuss I could get no reply." Donald was always notoriously difficult to pin down. Even, it seemed, for the good of the planet. Joking aside, the content of the letter shows his underlying commitment to the Yorkshire countryside.

Individuals show their passion for nature in many ways, and there are a lot of people in Yorkshire who now understand about conservation. Back on the farm of my friend Philip Shaw, who in an earlier chapter I was hoping would give me a little insight into how to retire gracefully, there are three beehives. When I last visited he briefly took the lid off one so I could take a peak. We'd just been discussing a nasty parasitic mite called *Varroa destructor* that can wipe out a whole colony, and I wanted to see if Philip's bees had been affected. They were fine. As we inspected the bees, Philip told me how he had begun beekeeping a few years before, after learning the basics on a short course. George Birks, a nearby elderly beekeeper who'd been getting rid of a few hives, showed Philip some of his bees, kitted him out with a protective outfit and began teaching him how to look after them. "Even now I occasionally stop and think: what would George do?" said Philip.

George, who'd worked in a bank before retiring, had been introduced to beekeeping by an uncle as a child in the 1920s. Thus began a lifelong fascination. George went on to keep thousands of bees, and became chairman of beekeeping associations around the country. He understood better than most the importance of these creatures in the cycle of life; they are not just about honey.

"Almost everything we eat is dependent on bees pollinating the crops," George told a newspaper in 2013, not long before he died. "If honey bees were to die out I don't know what would happen to the human population."

In fact, bees are said to pollinate 70 out of the 100 or so crop species that feed 90 percent of the world. As far as important species go, bees are at the top of the list, but they are vanishing from Britain. The environmental campaigning community Friends of the Earth has said we've lost 97 percent of our wildflower meadows since the 1930s, places where bees thrive. Scientists believe that if current trends continue, some species will simply disappear from Britain altogether.

What's the point of telling you all these stories about the natural world and the admirable individuals doing their best to preserve it? That's an easy one to answer: if I don't raise the issue, and we don't do something together, then all that we love could disappear. The environment can be destroyed very quickly, and if you don't believe me, take a walk in Rosedale, one of the most beautiful valleys in the North York Moors. Today it's a peaceful place to contemplate the world – the picture of how people imagine rural life to be in Yorkshire. Sheep, cows and horses graze in fields that rise up from the River Seven, which runs from the Moors down to the valley bottom. Visitors can hear the call of a curlew, and if they are lucky they might spot a deer. The noise of a tractor is one of the few man-made sounds. But that's not how it used to be; during the second half of the 19th century Rosedale was a busy industrial hub. Anyone visiting back then would have been confronted with noise, fumes, and hundreds of men busy mining and processing iron ore.

You don't have to be particularly observant to see what Rosedale used to be. There's an abandoned railway track that was built to take the iron ore out; it now provides a spectacularly elevated pathway for walkers and cyclists. There are also the crumbling remains of giant kilns, where the iron ore was roasted to remove impurities and reduce its weight, making it cheaper to cart away. The kilns were built into the hillside with giant stones and bricks. They are now deserted and falling apart. They look like what's left of giant temples built to praise a forgotten god, which, in some respects, is true. When the iron ore industry went into decline at the beginning of the last century, Rosedale returned to what it was like before the workmen had moved in. For Rosedale, it was a happy ending. But the point I'm making is that the peace of the natural world can easily be destroyed, just as the quiet and beauty of Rosedale was once shattered. The valley has now recovered, but the world might not unless we take firm action now.

⌒⋰⊙ CHAPTER 9 ⊙⋱⌒

Sheepdogs and Bicycles

Tess didn't hesitate when she jumped out of the back of the truck. She shot off across the field directly towards three black-faced Swaledale sheep, which immediately began to run as they saw – or perhaps sensed – her coming.

"She shouldn't have done that," said her owner. But he wasn't worried. He had no reason to be. Ordinarily he wouldn't want a dog let loose in a field of sheep, he said, but seven-year-old Tess was no ordinary dog. She's a sheepdog, a beautiful black and white Border Collie who works every day, and clearly loves it. On this occasion she had literally hit the ground running, after jumping from the back of her owner's truck. Farmer Andrew Hunter soon regained control of his dog by putting his fingers in his mouth and whistling. To Tess, the differing lengths and pitches of the sounds he was making were commands, and she just knew what to do. She moved with purpose back and forth around the three hardy hill sheep, driving them into another field.

50-year-old Andrew was standing in the pouring rain, but he was working and so not too bothered about getting wet. Plus, seeing a sheepdog running across a field is always a sight to behold, what-ever the weather. Andrew was also content for another reason.

His home and place of work is in the Yorkshire Dales' valley of Wensleydale, a place of astonishing beauty, character and history. Andrew is used to his surroundings, but he's not lost sight of why visitors are so enthralled by the lush countryside. In the field he was standing in he could see several of those world-renowned dry stone walls as they sliced through a rich and rolling landscape of varying shades of green.

Turning his head just slightly, Andrew could see Bolton Castle about a mile away, big and tall and proud, with its flag flying in the breeze. The castle is a popular tourist attraction steeped in history. It's still owned by descendants of the Scrope family, who built the castle way back, in the late 1300s. Mary Queen of Scots was later held there for six months, although it was a rather luxurious imprisonment. It's said that she had a retinue of 50, including knights, servants and ladies-in-waiting. Furniture, tapestries and rugs were brought from elsewhere to make her stay more comfortable, and Mary seems to have spent much of her time getting her hair done.

That was all ancient history. Now, Andrew was manoeuvering Tess around the field. "Away to the right, Tess! That'll do, that'll do!" Andrew called out in between sounding out a range of whistles he'd learned decades ago from his father, Raymond. These told the dog to stop, walk on, or go left, right or straight on. Whistling, rather than a shout lost in the wind, is easier for Tess to hear, particularly when she's a field or two away. Andrew wanted her to take the three sheep into a field, collect another five, then bring all eight back to him. It's fascinating to see Andrew and Tess at work. It's so nice to watch these lithe animals moving purposefully around to a soundtrack of whistles. After a few minutes of concentrated effort, Tess brought the eight sheep to a standstill just a few feet away from

Andrew. She stood there, proud and panting. "There you are," she seemed to be saying. "Mission accomplished."

Andrew said she sometimes ignores his commands. "She's getting more like that as she gets older, getting a mind of her own," he said, although it is important for sheepdogs to think for themselves occasionally.

Andrew is reserved and modest, but he knows what he's doing when it comes to dogs. He doesn't shout about it, but he has won numerous awards, which, I'm glad to say, his wife Wendy is less reticent about pointing out. Later on, back at the farmhouse, she showed me Andrew's many rosettes and trophies. The family home is a converted barn in a blissful spot near the village of Redmire. You get to it by driving down what was, on this particular day, a sodden and muddy lane. It passes a beguiling 12th-century church, a beautiful building that would take anyone's mind off the mud.

The lane eventually leads to a long and winding track that has a cattle grid on it. In the spring, visitors must drive with extra caution because there are sheep dotted around on the grass on either side; sometimes new mothers shelter from the rain with their babies beneath huge trees. Andrew's home stands at the end of the track behind a gate. It's part of Hogra Farm, 200 acres that Andrew farms with his father. They have been tenant farmers on this piece of land since 1988. Before that they worked a farm in Coverdale, not far away: they have always lived in the Dales. This father and son pair look after 25 beef cattle and about 300 sheep: Swaledales, Bluefaced Leicesters, and North of England Mules. Raymond didn't grow up on a farm as Andrew did; his own father worked in a quarry. But his childhood playground was nonetheless a marvellous one, deep in the countryside and messing around in the shadow of Bolton Castle.

Cyclists join former professional rider Sean Kelly testing the first stage of Tour de Yorkshire. This section of the route runs from Pickering to Whitby.

Raymond and Andrew are experts when it comes to handling sheep, something that in the past brought them into the orbit of James Herriot. Neither knew Alf or Donald, but they both met Christopher Timothy and Robert Hardy, the actors who played them in the TV series *All Creatures Great and Small*. That came about because several of Raymond's dogs, including a litter of tiny puppies, appeared in the programme, and a lot of the filming for the series was done in Wensleydale. (The Herriot books were, of course, set in the Dales, even though most of the stories actually happened around Thirsk.)

Raymond and his cows would later appear in a 1990s documentary about Herriot's Yorkshire with the actor Christopher Timothy, but the farmer's initial involvement with the world of TV came about through his vet at the time, a smart man who wore bow ties called Jack Watkinson. He was a veterinary adviser for *All Creatures Great and Small* but was sometimes called upon to be on screen too. Unknown to viewers, when a skilful close-up shot of a vet at work was needed, it was often Jack's hands that were filmed.

Jack helped find animals for different episodes, and occasionally asked to borrow Raymond's collies, including Lassie, a black, white and tan dog who was one of Tess's ancestors. Raymond also played an important off-screen role when it came to shots of the sheep dogs. "There'd be actors all dressed up, but we 'ad to do all the whistling, out of shot," Raymond said. Another time the storyline required a dog with a piece of wood "stuck" in its mouth. Raymond's collie Roy was perfect for the part, but that was only to be expected: he was very bright, a fine specimen who won more than a few dog trials.

Of course, there's a saying in the entertainment world that warns against working with children and animals. The film crew often found out exactly how true that was. On more than one occasion they failed to grasp how hard it can be to get an animal to do what you want it to do just because someone's shouted, "Action!" One scene required two collies to play with one another in the middle of a field, but they wouldn't do what they were told. In the end, Raymond went to one side of the field with one dog and someone else went to the other side with the other dog.

"We let them go at the same time, and they ran off and 'met' in the middle of the field," recalled Raymond. "On TV it looked good; it looked like they were playing. But they were more or less just passing each other," he laughed. Raymond and the then-young Andrew fared better when they appeared as extras themselves, wearing old-fashioned clothes and caps; it's easier to teach a human new tricks, after all. They both laughed as they remembered how Andrew was told to have his hair cut for his appearance in a scene about a sheepdog trial. "He wasn't right keen," said Raymond. "I was a teenager," his son replied, trying to explain his reluctance to cut off his locks. "At least you were getting a haircut for nowt," added his father.

The two men work hard, as they have done all their lives, but they try to make time for some of the simpler things in life, like a cup of tea and a chat at Andrew's kitchen table, which is often filled with delicious rolls and biscuits. Two large and lovely photographs of Andrew and the ever-eager Tess at work together hang on the wall just above. But the two men know that most of their work is outside, whatever the weather – and today it was raining.

After stopping for a quick cuppa, this father-and-son team pulled on their wet weather gear and went back outside to check on the farm's collies, which were locked up in their kennels. They have to be fastened up much of the time, because otherwise they'd be constantly herding sheep. As well as Tess (the best one at the moment, said Andrew), there was Rose, Billy, Troy and Wisp. Also Sid, owned by Andrew's teenage son, and a jumping, noisy bundle of joy called Flash, a seven-week-old pup, who'd only just started on solid food. Another of Andrew's collies, 12-year-old Jess, mother of Tess, wasn't there; she was probably relaxing in a barn. She'd be keeping warm and out of the rain, said Andrew – she wasn't stupid.

Raymond is now in his 70s and, although his son does most of the work, he joined Andrew in the rain to help out. At least he was well wrapped up. You can't blame him for not wanting to sit indoors all day. This has been his way of life for a long time, since he started working on farms as a teenager. One of six children, he needed a job and his parents didn't mind what he did as long as he got one. He'd been interested in farming and animals as a little boy, often following around a farmer called Walter Bostock, who had collected milk using a donkey with churns on its back. When Raymond left school at 15 he worked for the Bostock family, milking by hand. It was about this time that he got his first collie dog, although he can't remember its name now. "He wasn't a right good 'un." But he soon got another, and began trying to train them. Something about the dogs and their interaction with their owners and sheep must have attracted him. Soon afterwards he found a job as a shepherd on a nearby farm, learning what to do by watching more experienced men. He's had about 50 dogs and unlike his son, uses a special whistle to call them. He still wears one on a cord around his neck, the first thing he puts on in the morning and the last thing he takes off at night. "It takes a long time to learn how to use 'em," he said. "Some never get going with 'em."

Raymond is happy that his son also wanted to take up farming, and he's even more proud that Andrew has made a real success of it. His ability to impress the judges at sheep trials is clear to anyone who watches him for just a few minutes as he effortlessly instructs his dog to move the sheep without stressing them out or injuring them. Innumerable shepherds and farmers before him have learned to harness a puppy's natural instinct to chase and even kill. They have channelled, shaped and bred that instinct so the dogs, in partnership with the shepherd, can drive the sheep anywhere they want. Andrew has taught countless dogs to pen and hold these woolly mammals, and then drive them from here to there and back again. In return, the dogs seem pleased to hear a few words of praise, and be fed and patted. But not all collies can become successful sheep dogs. "The instinct to do it has to be in them," said Andrew. Clearly Tess was one of those born to the role.

The type of farming carried out by Raymond and Andrew are part and parcel of the Yorkshire Dales; so much so that it's hard to think of the area without imagining dogs herding sheep. Seeing this visual feast on screen in programmes such as *All Creatures Great and Small* has enticed many millions of tourists down the years. Although the area is a little way from Thirsk, where my old boss Alf Wight lived and worked, the Dales is a part of Yorkshire that he came to know and love, eventually buying a cottage there. Most famously it's where he went with his wife Joan for a working honeymoon in November 1941. In those days, rural vets carried out a lot of testing for tuberculosis and Alf could not be spared from the practice, even for his honeymoon. Plus, as he said afterwards, as young newlyweds they didn't have the money to do anything exotic. That's why they spent a couple of nights at The Wheatsheaf, a 19th-century pub in the village of Carperby, about three miles from where Raymond and Andrew farm.

The Wheatsheaf is a charming pub, some of it as it would have been in Alf's day, but with some modern twists. Nowadays it has wifi, a small sign near the bar stating: "Bullshit corner" and an extension housing a few extra bedrooms to add to the original nine.

The place is managed by two thirty-something step-sisters from Essex, Claire Boulton-Lear and Emily Skelton. They took over from their parents (Claire's mum and Emily's dad) about a decade ago. The women are well aware of the Herriot link; even now, many visitors turn up because they're interested in the wartime honeymoon visit. Pub staff show them a brown leather visitors' book resting in a glass case at the back of a small, one-tabled snug – the space was where the bar was situated when Alf visited. The book is open at a page that shows who stayed at the pub over a number of weeks in 1941 and 1942. For anyone interested in James Herriot, there, in black and white, is the author's distinctive signature: J A Wight (he was James Alfred Wight). A few lines below, there is a more surprising entry: Greta Garbo, the famous Hollywood film star. She stayed in The Wheatsheaf in January, weeks after Alf and Joan, apparently having boosted wartime morale by entertaining troops at Catterick Garrison a few miles away. It was one of her last performances. It was at about that moment in her life that Greta Garbo decided to retire from acting, shunning publicity for a more private life.

I don't know what room the acting legend slept in. But it's amusing to think she could have stayed in the same room as the Wights, with its brass bedstead and view of village houses and glorious hills beyond. I only wish the three of them had stayed in the pub at the same time. Bumping into Greta over a pint of Theakston's bitter or at breakfast could have been a fabulous tale for the Herriot books. Occasionally, a visitor to the Wheatsheaf asks to stay in room number nine, where the Wights laid their heads almost 80 years ago. It now has a wooden four-poster bed and ensuite bathroom, but the view is much the same. Mostly, though, Herriot fans visit the pub to see a framed letter hanging on the wall of the lounge a few feet from an old inglenook fireplace. Alf wrote it to his parents a few days after his church wedding in Thirsk. He was just 25.

A copy of the letter was given to the pub by Alf's son, my great friend Jim. It's a fascinating piece of writing because it's warm and funny, and shows how Alf already had great skill with the pen. The letter is addressed to Alf's parents because they were not there to see him get married. In fact, apart from the bride and groom, there were only three other people at the wedding. Small and frugal ceremonies were common during the war years and, for obvious reasons, it wasn't so easy to travel around the country and get to them. But Alf's parents, who still lived in Scotland, were apparently reluctant to attend their son's special day for another reason: his mother didn't really approve of Joan. Like many mums, she didn't think the young woman was good enough for her son, and she was cross the marriage was going ahead before Alf was financially secure.

Jim presented the handwritten letter, five pages long, both sweet and heart-warming, to The Wheatsheaf a few years ago. Alf's decency and sense of humour are clear to see, but his sadness about his "Mother & Dad" not seeing him get hitched, or even contacting him, is plain too. "I've tried in vain to phone you," he wrote. He was worried because they'd sent no word, "not even a wire on the day",

A signpost on the North York Moors showing Tour de Yorkshire competitors the way.

adding: "I really am upset about it, as I hurried back to Thirsk on Saturday expecting to find some word from you. I only hope nothing is wrong and I'll be relieved when I hear from you."

Having given his parents the benefit of the doubt, Alf moved on to describe the nuptials, weaving in some light-hearted details of the "dashed cold" wedding day. "The Canon was a bit doddery," he wrote, "and asked me if I would take this woman to be my lawfully wedded husband!" He explained that after their 9am wedding he and Joan had breakfast at Donald's before travelling to Richmond, on the edge of the Dales. "The day by this time was glorious and we felt on top of the world," he said. The couple spent the day in the market town, going to the cinema in the evening. While they were inside, their car was broken into. Cigarettes and chocolate Joan had saved for the special occasion were stolen. The thief also took a pair of silk stockings and some towels and coat hangers. Alf neatly summed up the newlyweds' feelings but, in keeping with the rational and calm personality I came to know well, didn't vent his spleen. "We were tired by this time and it made us quite miserable," was all he said.

Alf had little time to enjoy himself; he had to get on with the TB testing, visiting rambling grey-stone farmhouses across Wensleydale and Coverdale. Joan, a secretary, helped her husband by keeping written notes of the work. The couple often didn't finish work until 9pm. It's hard to imagine newlyweds now being willing to spend their honeymoon like that. Joan was tired "trudging up and down the mountains and through the mire like a hero", Alf wrote, but he maintained that he was fine, as he was used to lots of exercise in his job. Farmers and their wives congratulated the Wights, feeding them, handing out homemade chutney and extending invitations to return at pig-killing time.

Of course, Alf wouldn't have been Alf if he hadn't written about meals he and Joan ate on their honeymoon. He always loved his food, and told his parents that The Wheatsheaf's grub "was amazing: kippers and bacon and eggs for breakfast, and always plenty of fresh butter and Wensleydale cheese." He was less impressed with the car he used to navigate the hills and country lanes. He said it "passed out on me several times". When the couple left, he added, "the staff of the Inn had to turn out to push us off." But Alf, again showing signs of his look-on-the-bright-side-nature, was not too irritated. "Some honeymoon!" he wrote, before adding: "It was grand out there in the hills in the sunshine and I'm jolly glad we went there."

In 1979, Alf published a non-fiction book, *James Herriot's Yorkshire*, which became a huge bestseller, even selling more than his previous books. It featured photographs and writing about some of Alf's favourite places. A few pages were dedicated to his honeymoon and the pub where he'd spent it, including a passage on the owner at the time, a lady called Mrs Kilburn, and her niece, Gladys. "Those two good ladies fed us like royalty," Alf wrote. Mary Slade, now in her 70s, has always lived in Carperby. Her maiden name was "Kilburn" and she used to work in The Wheatsheaf, just like her late Auntie Annie and cousin Gladys, Alf's pub ladies. "Auntie Annie always wore black," said Mary. "She was a brilliant cook." Annie and Gladys even served the Wights a delicious hot meal when they first arrived, despite the late hour, which not everyone would have done. Alf said he hadn't expected anything to eat at that time of day. I like to think the kindness of the Carperby pub women to the newlyweds on their first day of married life helped to make up for the theft of their cigarettes, chocolate and silk stockings.

Alf and Joan mixed work and pleasure when they visited the Dales in 1941, and increasingly that mix is what the area is all about. Thousands of people work in the Yorkshire Dales National Park. Not all of them are farmers; tourism is now a key source of income and jobs. The Herriot books and TV series definitely fuelled interest in North Yorkshire, parts of which began marketing themselves as "Herriot Country". Herriot biographer Graham Lord wrote that not too long after *All Creatures Great and Small* began, tourism in the area increased by nearly half. He believed that Alf and the series were responsible for the creation of 3,000 new jobs in the Dales, where much of the TV series was shot. Alf would have been blown away, I'm sure.

Today, the Dales receives about four million visitors a year. They add around £260 million pounds to the region's economy, and thousands of people are in work because those tourists need feeding and watering. Good old Alf. He wasn't even a Yorkshireman, but he's probably done more for the county's coffers and reputation than anyone.

Tourism helps create the money that allows the Dales to retain their unique look. People want to go there and see the same landscape that Alf saw in his day. That's why it's so important to continue attracting visitors. A few years ago there was a perfect example of the innovative thinking of those behind the promotion of Yorkshire and its Dales. The Tour de France is the world's largest annual sporting event and, as the name suggests, it's mostly based in France. But it often starts in another country, and in 2014 that was Britain. Yorkshire, to be precise. The event proved such a success that the following year the Tour de Yorkshire was launched. Riders see rolling hills, flat caps and curd tarts instead of the Alps, berets and quiches. The Yorkshire event has already become an epic not to be missed. It's not hard to see why cyclists and spectators enjoy the springtime race so much. It passes through an exceptional range of landscapes, offering something for everyone. Yorkshire has buzzing cities, glorious coastlines, rivers dotted with ancient towns, rugged moors and, of course, the sublime Dales. For a few days of the year, men and women in lycra take over our highways and byways.

I've had the pleasure of pedalling in the Dales myself. Jim and I had our own mini tour there about 35 years ago. We fastened our bikes to his car and drove to Wensleydale before cycling ten or so miles to Swaledale and back again. It was between Christmas and New Year and there was no traffic. That ends any similarity between our trip and trips by today's professional bikers. I was on a sit-up-and-beg bike; some might even call it a lady's bike. I had no helmet, nor was I wearing any lycra. In fact, Jim and I both wore rather fetching anoraks. Mine was navy blue; his was light green. He led the way on country roads on his much faster bike to the village of Askrigg, where we stopped off for lunch at the King's Arms, which was called The Drovers when it featured in the TV series *All Creatures Great and Small*. We had ham and eggs and a couple of pints. Another time, Jim and I, along with a friend called Bill, cycled several miles to West Scrafton in Coverdale where Alf and Joan had a cottage. Bill said his calf muscles were so taut they felt like piano wires. I didn't let on, but mine felt no better.

I rarely bike these days (cycling is another thing on my retirement list), but I love watching the Tour de Yorkshire. In 2019 it passed through one of the most beautiful villages in the Dales: Kettlewell, a perfect place to see cyclists whoosh past on what was stage four of the race, the last day.

It's a wonderful spot at any time of the year, with dry stone walls and stunning views. The village looks small next to its mesmerising backdrop, a jagged hill called Great Whernside, which rises up more than 2,300 feet. Where better to see superb athletes than this wonderful natural environment? The Dales are full to overflowing with ups and downs, some of them hard enough for walkers, let alone cyclists. On this stage, the riders would have to pedal up a hill called Park Rash, just outside Kettlewell. For Tour de Yorkshire day it had even been given a French name, "Côte de Park Rash", in a nod to the original Tour de France. Whatever you choose to call it, it's incredibly hard work moving up it under your own steam. It would be, without a doubt, 2.2km of intense legwork. Sacré bleu!

Spectators started arriving early in Kettlewell, even before the day's racing had begun. They wanted to soak up the atmosphere and find a good place to watch the race. The 175km stage that day was from Halifax to Leeds. Kettlewell was somewhere in the middle. As a handful of police officers mingled with the first tourists, a group of amateur cyclists went by. They were doing the Tour route a few hours before the professionals. A small group of walkers were amused when they overtook one of the cyclists as they all went up a hill – the man on the bike was going so slowly. Crows squawked above the blue and yellow bunting and woolly baubles that had been strewn across trees, walls and houses to decorate the village for the race. A middle-aged couple went past pushing a large straw horse along. They told a quizzical passerby that the animal was for the village's annual Scarecrow Festival in August. Had they got the date wrong? It was still only May.

In the village's grass and flower-filled churchyard, 70-year-old church volunteer Phil Burgin pointed out a centuries-old grave to a visitor. "Her grandfather was the first MP for Richmondshire," he said. Inside the almost empty church he showed off the Norman font, all that remains of the original building that went up in 1120. Phil used to be a fell runner and was a regular on Great Whernside, running up it for years at least once a month, whatever the weather. He can't do that these days, but he still walks and cycles. On Tour de Yorkshire day he was on a journey of his own: to check spectators didn't squash the yellow primroses on the grassy banks of Park Rash.

As a pilgrimage of people continued to arrive in Kettlewell, many of them armed with folding chairs, picnics and yapping dogs, the owner of Zarina's tearooms, Zarina Belk, prepared to watch the race. She remembered the excitement of the Tour de France in 2014 when it passed through the village even if, as she said, there was some confusion over road closures. "We'd been told to cater for thousands so we made loads of food, but the customers couldn't really get here so a lot went to waste." It's true to say, though, that the event, and the Yorkshire version since, have certainly encouraged people to visit the Dales. "We get a lot of men in lycra," Zarina said with a grin. Including, occasionally, Olympic triathlon champions the Brownlee brothers.

Staging a bike ride through the exquisite scenery of the Yorkshire Dales is perhaps an obvious way to attract more tourists to the area, but sometimes the things that bring in visitors are not so easy to spot, something Zarina knows all about. The teashop owner knows a group of mature women who, unexpectedly, created worldwide excitement twenty years ago by taking part in an unusual fund-raising exercise. I know a few of them myself. These lovely ladies were part of a Women's Institute in the nearby hamlet of Rylstone. While trying to think of a way to raise money to fight cancer after the death of John Baker, the husband of one of them, they hit on the idea of stripping off to shoot a saucy calendar. For them, there were no photographs of wondrous sunsets or flower-filled paths. Instead, the women, including Mr Baker's widow Angela, were snapped in the nude, their modesty hidden by strategically-placed items associated with traditional Women's Institute pursuits, such as baking and sewing.

The ladies, aged between 45 and 66, hoped to raise a few thousand pounds. No one could have had an inkling of the media frenzy that would follow the calendar's publication, with coverage in newspapers, and on TV and radio, around the globe. Even the Queen and Queen Mother were interested; some of the Yorkshire women travelled down to London to give copies of the calendar to them. Australians and Americans were among the many people jamming hotlines, desperate to get their hands on pictures of naked ladies from the Dales. Millions of pounds have been raised.

The calendar's fame also brought more tourists to the area, with many more arriving after a film of the women's antics – *Calendar Girls* – came out in 2003. It stars world-famous actresses Julie Walters and Helen Mirren. Parts of it were shot in Kettlewell, and Zarina was an extra in one of the scenes. But her links to the story are also very personal. She not only knows the calendar women, she also knew John. Her mother worked with him at the Dales' National Park office in the nearby village of Grassington. On a wall of the tearoom is a large photo of the café's reopening party a decade or so ago after a refurbishment. Zarina is grinning broadly, along with Angela and five other Calendar Girls, this time all fully clothed. One of them, Ros (Miss November in the original calendar) worked for Zarina as a cook for a while. Ros proved particularly popular with American tourists. "They thought they'd met their dream when they came into contact with a real Calendar Girl."

In 2012 Zarina herself stripped off on stage in the world amateur premiere of the play about the women's story. The play had already been hugely successful in the West End and on tour before it was opened up to amateurs. Because the Dales was the home of the real Calendar Girls, Zarina and the rest of the local cast were given permission to perform one night before any other amateur performances. Promotional photographs showed the ladies naked in the Dales. They wore pearls and walking boots, their scripts and a map hiding what they didn't want people to see. Zarina played a character called Ruth, based on Ros. At one point she had to sit on a table with a few marmalade jars covering her private parts and "the biggest wooden spoon you have ever seen covering my right boob. My arm covered the other one."

There's a musical now too, the music written by none other than Gary Barlow, former Take That frontman. And, in a touching postscript, John's widow Angela fell in love with an old university friend and married him.

Back outside on the streets of Kettlewell, more crowds of fun-loving spectators and lycra-clad amateur cyclists had appeared and a carnival atmosphere was starting to build. Inside the Blue Bell Inn that was built in 1680 (it's one of the oldest buildings in Kettlewell – many others were destroyed in a 1686 flood), people were queuing as bar staff took orders for pints, sticky toffee puddings and Sunday lunches. One male server got cross with a lady who politely queried where her desserts were. "Don't you know it's the Tour today?" he barked. Someone wondered if a man called Daniel Ambler would dare to show his face again, as on a blue plaque were these words: "On this spot, Daniel Ambler admitted he was wrong, 15th December, 2013". Old photographs gave tantalising hints of times gone by, showing farmers and their families next to bales of hay and smartly dressed drivers of early cars. In one picture, a lone woman sat on a seat outside, staring into space, her long skirt trailing around her legs.

Tragedy was framed for posterity too; one typewritten note explained how the Blue Bell's 1914 landlord, Private William Henry Townson, had been wounded twice in the First World War before being captured by the Germans. He never returned home, dead at 42. Near the toilets at the back of the Blue Bell there was a mention on the wall of the well-known Yorkshire novelist and playwright JB Priestley, probably best known for his 1945 play *An Inspector Calls*. In *English Journey*, his 1930s book about the state of the nation during the Great Depression, he mentioned how far people were prepared to walk in the Bradford of his childhood. He said they thought nothing of tramping between thirty and forty miles every Sunday. He was so fond of the Dales his ashes were buried there, not far from Kettlewell.

JB Priestley is once supposed to have asked a local woman why she no longer went to Kettlewell. She replied that she "couldn't stand t'racket". She would have hated Tour day. Outside the Blue Bell, a few metres away from a small stone bridge, the noise was increasing by the minute. There were no tables left and people stood sipping their pints in the sunshine while children and dogs occasionally whined at their feet. A Tour volunteer, a retired GP called Terry in a high-viz vest, stood in the road directing spectators and prepared to use his flag and whistle when the race finally made its appearance. "The cyclists will come over the bridge and hear me, then spot me pointing to where they need to go," he said. He, and others like him, were certainly needed; the cyclists spend a lot of time with their heads down, looking at the backside of the person in front.

Terry was also on the lookout for protestors. There'd been some elsewhere, complaining about the British team's switch from Team Sky to Team Ineos. Some had gathered outside the team's bus on the first day of the race, criticising the chemical company Ineos for its links to fracking and plastic production. In Kettlewell, a few men and women, part of a group called Yorkshire For Europe, held up EU flags while they waited for the race to pass through. "Let down by Downing Street – not Brussels" was their motto. Someone said they might get more publicity if they were naked, just like the Calendar Girls.

Finally a caravan of vehicles arrived, the first with a big yellow "Y" on it to represent Yorkshire. In a frenzy of tooting horns they pulled up by the pub, and their grinning occupants emerged to hand out freebies to the crowd. Most items were appreciated, some not so much. To whoops and laughs, packets of instant noodles, small plastic cows and big foam fingers were thrust into grasping hands. Some smaller children were disappointed, thinking they were getting sweets. Some adults were also disappointed: they thought they were getting free shots of gin. On a hill just outside the village, with a view of pretty homes, fields and farms, spectators stood or sat watching the vehicles go by. For some reason, the 1980s song *Take On Me*, by the Norwegian band A-ha, was playing as a cyclist with a small dog in the front basket rode by.

Then came several amateur riders, a car with two bikes on its roof, and a few police motorcyclists. One officer with a moustache went by twice – or maybe he had a twin. A little girl moved a worm from the country road, out of harm's way for two seconds before it was trodden on by a man kicking a stone away. Dogs barked; some went berserk. One Bedlington Terrier suddenly laid down in a stranger's lap. People bantered and ate sandwiches. Some were tipsy. The Driskell family from Cheshire, who were camping near-by, were excited, especially five-year-old Emily. Clutching her toy bunny, she said she'd only just learned how to ride a bike.

At the sight of the helicopter, up in the air filming the Tour, the noise of the crowd started to rise. A little boy, waving like mad in the hope he'd be on TV, fell off his deckchair. Then, at about 2.40pm, a group of professional cyclists, nine of them, powered up the hill. It was the leading pack. None had to get off and push, as Jim and I would have probably had to do. Everyone cheered and waved and screamed as the helicopter hovered.

Then the men were gone, just as quickly as they had arrived. Soon afterwards, a bigger group of cyclists came by. Then they were gone too. A couple of ambulances came into view before a car with another big yellow "Y" on top appeared. All that was needed was a big full stop to follow, because that was it. Hours of waiting for a few minutes of action. But there didn't seem to be any disappoint-ment at the brevity of the spectacle. After all, this was the Yorkshire Dales. Whatever reason people come for, there would always be the scenery to look at.

CHAPTER 10

Market Day

I t was 7.45am on a Monday morning in April and, although the tree blossoms and flowers suggested warmth to come, it was still cold enough for a hat and plenty of layers. The coffee Carl Anderson was sipping warmed him up, as did his black fingerless gloves. In fact, he was so wrapped up and busy he wasn't really registering the chill in the air. It was market day in Thirsk and although Carl had been hard at it since he heaved himself out of bed at 12.30am (yes, 12.30am), there was still a lot to do before the morning properly kicked off.

Carl's Flowers, Fruit and Veg often does a roaring trade, especially when there are tourists as well as locals to serve, with at least 60 percent of his produce – including beetroot, parsnips and leeks – grown in Yorkshire.

On this particular day, the cold weather would probably keep some people at home. There certainly wouldn't be the crowds you get on a bank holiday or a race day, although that didn't seem to bother Carl. He was as chipper as usual. He took over the stall a few years ago, but has been selling fruit and veg one way or another for 40 years, since he was about 11. He now trades at various markets in the locality, delivers direct to pubs and restaurants, and runs a

400-acre farm. I don't know how he survives on just four hours' sleep a night but, considering what he has to do, it's probably a miracle he gets that much. "Four hours is enough for anyone," he said, with a bluntness you expect in these parts.

It was still early and so the market square was mostly quiet, apart from a few pedestrians and the odd motorist. One of the few people out and about was a young man sitting on the steps of the Victorian clock tower, smoking and watching the stallholders laying out their wares on cobbles in front of The Golden Fleece pub. This historic building, long a drinking haunt for us vets, has been a silent witness to this Monday spectacle for centuries. It describes itself as a "hotel, eatery and coffee house", but probably started off as a private house. Parts of it date back to the 1500s, including a big, oak-beamed inglenook fireplace.But however old the Fleece might be, it's a mere sapling compared to the market itself, which has been a feature of Thirsk since 1145. Think about all that time: nearly nine centuries. And think about everything that has ever been sold in this modest space. It makes my head spin. On this particular morning, stalls had been quickly set up, with everything enticingly laid out to encourage as many people as possible to part with their hard-earned cash. It was clear that Carl the veg man and his team of ladies, young and old, knew exactly what they were doing. Watching them at work was like watching a well-oiled machine. His most experienced employee, Evelyn Hebdon, was in her 80s. She first got involved with the stall as a teenager. It was her grandad who started it up, back in 1898. He had a horse and cart and sold seeds.

The first customers soon started to arrive, chatting among stalls selling everything from duvets and car mats to toilet rolls, wine gums and dog biscuits. Former mechanic Mohinder Singh Birdi, now in his mid-60s, pulled ladies' clothes from his van and hung them neatly on racks. Something blew away; a passer-by picked up whatever it was and handed it to him with a smile. Mr Birdi, also the treasurer of a Sikh temple in Leeds, took over the stall from his brother when he retired. The family has worked in Thirsk's market since 1973 and have been serving some customers for decades. Mr Birdi was born at the top of India, so that's something we have in common: we're both northerners. He was 11 when he arrived in Britain, and barely spoke a word of English. But he quickly mastered the language and adapted to life in this alien land, even getting to grips with the Yorkshire accent, or accents. There are certainly similarities between the country of his early childhood and the one he adopted long ago. "Many people like to barter in India too," he grinned.

If the market and its stallholders are essential ingredients of Thirsk, it struck me anew that the countryside around it has also contributed to its character. Like a hand in a glove, Thirsk nestles beautifully in the centre of the Vale of Mowbray. With the Hambleton Hills to the east and the Yorkshire Dales to the west, the town is surrounded by acre upon acre of fertile grazing land. Thirsk has been a busy hub for the local area for more than 1,400 years, a centre for trade and business for the nearby villages, hamlets and farms, including Thirkleby and Topcliffe where I grew up. It was also a staging post for the Great North Road, the main thoroughfare running from London to Scotland, as well as more local routes to the likes of Ripon and Scarborough. So the place has always been both local and national, a small town intimately connected to the rhythms of the people who live there, but also one with links to the world outside.

Thirsk market place on market day circa 1955. People from the outlying villages would travel into town on coaches.

Of course, the history and the significance of Thirsk is something I came to only later. When I first got to know the town, when I was just a child, it was simply somewhere I used to go shopping with my family. At that age, Thirsk for me was about toys, sweets and comics. Later, I went to secondary school there, obviously a very important time in a young life.

But Thirsk will always be the place where I first realised I wanted to become a vet. At 23 Kirkgate, a building just off the market-place and home to the practice run by Alf Wight, his son Jim, and Donald Sinclair, I started to become the person I am today. My former colleague, the practice's secretary Joan Snelling, is in her 70s now, but can clearly remember me arriving for my first day on work experience, when I was still at school. I was a very shy teenager, but one of my favourite teachers, a man called John Ward, knew the Wights well and arranged for me to spend time at their practice. It was a day that set me on my current course.

It's all a bit of a blur now, but I must have managed to walk up the steps, go through the big red front door and introduce myself to Joan. She went to get Alf, or Mr Wight as she always called him, who was expecting me. That everyday moment, right there, was the start of the rest of my life. Almost immediately I fell head over heels in love with Kirkgate, its staff and the work. Soon I was regularly going out on calls with Alf and the other vets, taking every opportunity to find out all I could about caring for sick and injured animals. A few years later, I went to university to study veterinary medicine, but it wasn't long before I found my way back to Thirsk.

The Kirkgate practice became as familiar to me as my own hands. I went up and down the three steps to the front door almost every day during the many years I worked there. Inside, I would witness life and death, goodwill and humour. The click of the latch as you entered the building was one of the many things I missed when we moved to our new surgery, Skeldale, in 1996, on the outskirts of Thirsk. 23 Kirkgate is now a museum, to showcase the books and way of life that Alf wrote about as James Herriot. But whenever I go back and walk on the original hall tiles and hear that iconic click, I'm taken right back to my teenage years and my 20s when I was really getting to know the place.

Alf's first impressions of Thirsk were equally strong. He was born in Sunderland but grew up in Glasgow and didn't know much about the town before moving there to work in 1940. He came to love Thirsk and Yorkshire dearly in the years that followed, and even fictionalised his arrival for the very first time in his 1970 book, *If Only They Could Talk*. He talks about getting out of a "rickety little bus" in "Darrowby", his fictional name for Thirsk. This is how he describes it:

"I got out and stood beside my battered suitcase, looking about me. There was something unusual and I couldn't quite put my finger on it at first. Then I realised what it was – the silence. The other passengers had dispersed, the driver had switched off his engine and there was not a sound or movement anywhere. The only visible sign of life was a group of old men sitting round the clock tower in the centre of the square, but they might have been carved from stone."

Alf went on to say that Darrowby didn't get much space in the guidebooks. Not anymore, and to a large extent it was James Herriot himself and his fame that made sure of that. Tourists have come in their droves over the years. The square with its old cobbles and clock tower are still there, but the silence has gone (unless, of course, it's 3am when most people are tucked up in bed). Despite the changes, though, Thirsk retains much of the beauty of Herriot's Darrowby.

I can easily get myself worked up when I remember one particular teacher I didn't like at school. He once upset me by saying how useless we were in Thirsk. "The tide flows in and ebbs out again, and where it turns it leaves a load of rubbish on the beach. That's Thirsk," he'd laugh. I bet he wouldn't laugh if he saw how lovely, and how popular, the town is today.

The town gave Alf many of the characters for his book. I'm always reminded of that fact when I go past the late Marjorie Warner's Edwardian home, Thorpe House, just a few minutes' walk from the town centre. Mrs Warner's larger-than-life character was known in the Herriot books and on screen as Mrs Pumphrey. She's loved by millions through Alf's writing, and tourists can see a mannequin of her in the Herriot museum. The wealthy widow treated her Pekinese dog (Tricki Woo in the Herriot books) like royalty, and immortalised some of his ailments with her vivid descriptions. "Flop bott" was what she said when her pooch's anal glands needed emptying; "cracker dog" was how she described it when he went berserk, running madly all over the place. Young Alf (Uncle Herriot) visited the pair regularly and was often sent hampers of fine food from Tricki Woo.

Apart from the tasty delicacies and warm welcome he received, I can easily understand why Alf enjoyed visiting Thorpe House. The building and grounds are stunning, and there's a first-rate view of the Hambleton Hills. Mrs Warner even bought a nearby field to preserve the view. Since 1993, her old home has been part of Holy Rood House, a charity and retreat offering a "safe space for those of us who are finding life unsafe." Alf, a kind man who sometimes struggled with his mental health and later became a Samaritan, would have found that rather fitting.

Naturally, most tourists want to know all about Mrs Pumphrey's house, along with all the other locations associated with James Herriot – many "ginnels", or alleyways, full of old housing, among them. This has ultimately brought a lot of money to the town and wider area. But, important as Alf was and still is to Thirsk, there is much more to "Herriot country" than the Herriot connections. Our brilliant tourism volunteers who show visitors around love to talk about our famous vet and author, but they also relish telling other tales with unexpected connections to Thirsk. I only recently found out, for example, that in 1797, when Lord Nelson was wounded in the battle with the Spanish for Tenerife, his right arm was amputated by the Thirsk-born surgeon Thomas Eshelby.

I also love the story about the Giant of Castle Garth, a green expanse of land just west of the marketplace. I often played there with my mates when I was still at school. It was on that spot, when workers were building an electrical substation 25 years ago, that they uncovered several early Saxon graves. An analysis of some of the bones found on the site showed they were from a man almost seven feet tall. What a height. Some of his bones are on display in the town's museum. I occasionally wonder about the Giant's descendants when I see a tall local, of which I am one.

Castle Garth is still often used by dog walkers and as a play area for kids but, as its name suggests, it once played a more important part in Thirsk's history. The Normans built a castle there after their conquest of England, and at one point it fell into the hands of a man called Roger de Mowbray, the kind of swashbuckling knight that seems to dominate history books. He lived a colourful life. He was known as a brilliant fighter, but sometimes managed to find himself on the losing side. In the 1170s he rebelled against King Henry II and had to surrender. The castle was destroyed. Luckily, Roger fared a little better and was pardoned by the king. Later on, he went to fight in a Crusade to the Holy Land, but was captured and died in circumstances that have never been fully explained. Considering the time that has elapsed between then and now, we will probably never know the true story.

Thirsk's history is choc-a-bloc with interesting people. One of my personal favourites is Thomas Parkinson, who had an unusual home at St Mary's Church on Kirkgate, just along the road from my old practice. The church is the place where Alf and his sweetheart Joan – Helen in the Herriot books – were married during the Second World War. This Gothic building, more than 500 years old, is one of Thirsk's oldest, and Thomas Parkinson was for a while the church's resident hermit. He apparently lived alone in a small room above the porch in the 1500s so he could see if he was cut out for monastic life. There was no staircase up to his unusual lodgings back then. Thomas needed a rope ladder to climb up to his door, set high in the wall. Kind townsfolk brought him food and drink. Thomas later became a monk at Mount Grace Priory, about 12 miles away, so his trial run at St Mary's obviously went well.

Occasionally, Thirsk has thrown up a character who has had more than a passing influence on the world outside our small town. Thomas Lord is one. His contribution centres on the game that has become inextricably linked to Yorkshire. I'm talking, of course, about cricket, a game I love, but was never very good at. Born in 1755, Thomas became a professional player of a game that was then still in its infancy. History suggests he was a decent bowler, but it wasn't on the field of play that he left his mark. His fame came through his association with a short-lived team known as the White

Conduit Club. In 1786 a group of aristocrats who played for the club asked Thomas to find them a ground to play on. They eventually settled on what is now simply known as Lord's, the hallowed turf in north London that is still the spiritual home of cricket and its most famous venue, a venue where, almost unbelievably, England won the World Cup against New Zealand on 14 July 2019. It was probably the greatest cricket match ever played. We can only wonder what Thomas might have thought of that nail-biting game at Lord's. At least we can find out more about the man himself in a museum on Kirkgate, located in the house where he was born. It's a real gem.

However, the museum, which opened in 1977, is about much more than the history of cricket. It's a true Tardis of interesting and unusual items, one of which is an innocuous-looking wooden chair hanging on a wall. It might look ordinary, but it has a very dark history. Back in 1702, a man called Thomas Busby, a bully and drunkard who made coins, was accused of murdering his father-in-law by bludgeoning him to death. He was found guilty and sentenced to death by hanging. On the way to his execution he cursed anyone who dared to sit in "his" chair at the Thirsk inn where he used to drink. Thomas' corpse was suspended in chains on a stoop, a kind of post, near the inn, which later became known as the Busby Stoop Inn, taking its name from both the dead man and the place where his body was displayed.

The drinking establishment, now an Indian restaurant, was said to be haunted by Busby's ghost, with one particular chair gaining a sinister reputation. Bomber pilots during the war said it was unlucky to sit on it. It was said that those who dared to do so did not return from their missions. Fatal accidents were also linked to the chair. A hitchhiker was supposedly knocked down and killed after trying it out for size, and a builder's apprentice who sat in it one lunchtime fell to his death from a roof that same afternoon. In 1978, after banishing the chair to the cellar, the pub landlord gave it to the museum on the condition that no one ever sat in it. That's why it's hung up on the wall, out of harm's way.

"Last year I had four or five emails, including messages from Pakistan and America, asking to buy the chair," said Jim Seymour, a retired biology teacher who is chairman of the museum's management committee and lives next door to my *Yorkshire Vet* colleague Julian. An American collector offered to pay a million pounds for the chair, notes from Russia pop up from time to time saying money is no object, and it's been filmed by TV crews from as far away as Japan. "People also offer to pay to sit in the chair, but they are never allowed to," added Jim. He thinks the deaths associated with the chair are just coincidences, but even so: "I still wouldn't sit in it." I wouldn't either.

Inevitably, the museum contains a few items connected to James Herriot, which are kept in a small box that Jim Seymour has in his office. Inside are two of Alf's original Herriot manuscripts: *It Shouldn't Happen To A Vet* and *Let Sleeping Vets Lie*, his second and third books. Alf donated the typewritten scripts to the museum in 1978. Flicking carefully through them, enjoying handling their cardboard covers and imagining Alf doing the same, you can see a few handwritten corrections. On one page the original typed words "with my boss Siegfried" have been changed in pen to read "with my gifted but mercurial boss Siegfried". The change was kept when the book went to print, a better phrase to capture Donald's unpredictable changes of mood and mind. Also in the box is an out-of-focus snapshot of Alf and Donald with the actors Anthony

Hopkins and Simon Ward, taken in a break during shooting for the 1975 film *All Creatures Great and Small* (yes, there were films as well as the TV series). The four men are all smiling as they lean on a fence, obviously enjoying one another's company, with Anthony standing between my two old bosses, his arm resting on Donald's shoulder.

Of course, all this history was neither here nor there when I first started working as a vet. I was just interested in learning as much as I could about the job. Mind you, there was one aspect of my day that I always looked forward to that had nothing to do with work: lunchtime, or dinner time as we say in Yorkshire. I looked forward to it because I'd usually go to my Granny Duncalf's to eat. She lived nearby. Alf's son Jim, also a vet, sometimes came too. We'd be starving by the time we arrived, especially if we'd had a hard morning out and about on a farm chasing energetic calves around. The tantalising smell of my granny's home-cooked food would hit us as soon as we walked through the door. Her stews, roast beef dinners and rice puddings were legendary in my family, and Jim's appreciation was clear from his many second helpings. Granny also stuffed us both with freshly baked bread, scones and cakes, while we'd talk between mouthfuls about what we'd been up to.

Places in Thirsk at that time were known to me mainly because of the animals I treated who lived in them. I've naturally dealt with hundreds, if not thousands of patients over the years, but there's one I've never forgotten because it was such a sad and unusual case. It involved a golden retriever that had died of old age, leaving behind its companion, another retriever. After the loss of her friend, the remaining dog started sleeping most of the time, and stopped eating. I ran some tests, but couldn't find anything physically wrong with her. I had to conclude that she was basically in mourning for her friend. It was weeks before she recovered. It was the worst case of bereavement I've ever seen in an animal.

I think of this sad canine if I go to the Three Tuns pub in the marketplace. The two dogs had lived there happily with their doting owners, pub landlords Daphne and Ivan Redman. Whenever a vet walked in for a pint, they would always start barking (the dogs, not the owners), even before they'd laid eyes on us. It happened a lot because I used to drink in the pub quite a bit, even though there was always the chance of an unwelcome encounter from an unhappy client. I remember one incident in particular.

"Peter, d'you remember that cow you came to see, week before last?" a farmer shouted across the bar, while Jim and I tried to have a quiet drink. I did remember, and closed my eyes as I waited for the punchline. "It were stiff as a board following mornin'," the farmer said, staring intently at me, his eyes penetrating my soul. I was left feeling utterly miserable. Jim, head down, was just relieved he hadn't been picked on this time around.

I can't help but associate Thirsk with the people who lived there or who visited its pubs, shops and market. And you can believe me that the town has nurtured some very interesting folk down the years. Take Bill Foggitt, for example. He was a descendant of William Jackson Foggitt, who founded a chemist's in Thirsk in 1836. It was in business for just over a century, until it was purchased by Boots. The Foggitts were magistrates, Methodists and preachers, and through an interest in meteorology built up a vast body of weather observations. This gave 20th-century descendant Bill Foggitt plenty of data for his famous appearances on television as a weather pundit in the 1980s. Foggitt's Forecasts were, for some, more respected than predictions from the Meteorological Office. Bill's ability to predict the weather was based on his family's observations of nature made over 200 years. Instead of using powerful computers, Bill would decide what the weather would be the following day by looking at, say, the erratic behaviour of sheep. He was also passionate about what seaweed could tell him. "When air is getting damp, that's a sign that rain is not far off," he would say, then explain that a damp atmosphere acted on the salt inside the seaweed, which then became damp and straggly. "If the air is dry, the seaweed goes brittle and hard," he often said. "Seaweed's probably the best way of forecasting. The only problem is that I'm too far from the coast in Thirsk to get hold of much."

I often saw Thirsk's very own weather prophet in the practice with his little terrier, or the pair of them in the pub where Bill would be having a quiet pint. Then I'd see him on TV the next day. He died in 2004, but I still think of him if I'm passing Boots, where there's a commemorative blue plaque for him. Sometimes his predictions were very accurate. It's a shame he isn't around anymore: as well as being a much-missed character, it would be fascinating, if a little scary, to hear his thoughts on our current weather patterns.

Unsurprisingly, there's plenty of our great Yorkshire dialect to be heard bouncing around the cobbles and streets of Thirsk. But in this age of globalisation the name James Herriot continues to spread far and wide and folk from all over the world come to the town.

Occasionally you can hear a language more usually heard inside the walls of the Kremlin. As strange as it might sound, there's a thriving group of Herriot fans in Russia, and more than a few of them make it to God's own country. In fact, so many have visited over the last few years that the Herriot Museum now employs its own Russian speaker to show them round. Alfiya Stephenson is the woman charged with this job. I suppose it's no surprise that there are Herriot fans in Russia. There has barely been a year since the 1970s that *All Creatures Great and Small* has not been shown on TV there. There are fan clubs that regularly meet up to watch and discuss reruns of the series. Episodes with Russian voice-overs and subtitles are even available on YouTube.

And there's another connection between James Herriot and Russia. In 1961, Alf was given the chance to work on a ship sailing to Lithuania, in what was then the Soviet Union. It came about because one of his friends, John Crooks, was often the on-board vet for animals being transported to Eastern Europe. Seeing how interested Alf was, he managed to get him on one of the sailings. His job on board the ship from Hull, as I briefly mentioned in an earlier chapter, was to look after 383 pedigree sheep, worth £20,000, a massive sum at the time. It was no small responsibility but, as Alf wrote 20 years later in his book *The Lord God Made Them All*: "Country vetting is fine, but sometimes I feel I'm sliding into a rut. A trip to Russia is just what I need". Many of his clients didn't agree. After all, East-West relations were at a low ebb. But Alf fancied a big adventure so, aged 45, off he went.

The rural vet managed to keep his sea legs, despite a force-nine gale, continuing to eat and drink with gusto as he always did, tucking into the chef's gourmet food while experienced sailors went green around the gills. But it wasn't all plain sailing. After disembarking in the port of Klaipeda, he decided he wanted to make a trip into town, and looked for a shortcut. It was dark, and a massive Alsatian-type dog, barking and snarling, suddenly appeared out of nowhere and went for him. Alf tried to run, then tripped and fell. The only reason the animal was unable to tear his throat out was because it was on a chain too short for it to reach its flailing human prey. Alf later wrote: "I felt I had learned my first lesson. Do not go nosing about in dark places in Russia. Keep to the proper path." Luckily, the evening turned out fine. Alf and his companion, the ship's Danish captain, managed to find the place they were looking for, a seamen's club, and enjoyed a convivial evening.

For me, Thirsk is all these things: my childhood, my career, and my friends and colleagues. It's the history, slowly absorbed over decades of life, and a gradual realisation of how important the town is to the surrounding area.

Thirsk was here long before I arrived, and will be here long after I'm gone. I certainly hope the market will still be up and running in centuries to come. Back with the stallholders on that cold April Monday it was early afternoon and Tony Cox, of Tony's Grimsby Fish, was starting to pack up. Not that his day was over; he usually drives about 12 miles to a pub in Boroughbridge after he's done in Thirsk, not for a pint, but for customers who meet him there to look over what's left of his stock. This former wardrobe fitter in his clean white apron (that day, he had on a black body warmer and striped woolly hat too) has been a regular fixture in the market for more than a decade. He gets up in his Grimsby home at 2.30am to rub the sleep from his eyes, pull on his clothes and drive to the docks, where his late father was an electrician. There he buys mini mountains of moist fresh fish, their eyes still shiny, including haddock, cod and salmon, but also more exotic fare such as tuna from South America.

Tony spends several hours on the road, four days a week. Despite his hectic schedule, he's usually chipper and engaged, easily remembering what his regular customers want. He sees them coming, and their fish is often being bagged up before they even reach his van. "I cook fish three times a week, often sea bass," he told one woman who'd said she wasn't a great cook. "Do everything else, like your veg, first," he said. "The fish needs just five minutes on the skin side, four minutes on the other side."

Nearby, a small crowd had gathered around a farmer's daughter, known as Ruth to her customers. She's tall, in her early 60s, and wears a straw hat on top of her long hair. That afternoon she was sitting in front of her Thirsk stall playing the guitar her father gave her when she was 12, and singing at top speed. She often sings when she sells her homemade fare, known as Winnie's Yorkshire Delights. "If you buy something you get a song," she told a passer-by. She has jar upon jar of chutneys and jams, all made without additives or artificial colours in her kitchen. She's won awards for her beetroot relish, made according to her late mother's recipe.

She wasn't the only one feeling musical. A grey-haired man wearing glasses had popped up near Ruth and begun playing a piano accordion, its case open next to him for coins from anyone inclined to show their appreciation. It turned out he lived in Otley, about 35 miles away, and usually played there. It's not often you hear such an instrument in Thirsk's marketplace, and it's probably fair to say it's not often you see a retired copper playing one either. For the man bashing out the tunes was a former deputy chief constable called Adrian Ward. Having played the accordion since he was a boy, he now composes his own songs and performs at parties. He even played at his son's wedding. "This is far better than being a policeman," said the 63-year-old during a brief pause. It was his first time busking at Thirsk market and, nine centuries after shoppers first started coming here, visitors happily went about their business to the sound of his peaceful melodies.

CHAPTER 11

The Ups and Downs of York

Of course, Yorkshire has bigger places than Thirsk, and York is a particular favourite. I don't get much chance to visit very often, so was pleased I had an appointment to see some of the work of Street Paws, a charity I'm involved with that provides free veterinary care to animals owned by people who are homeless or in vulnerable housing. But I'd also allowed myself a little free time to look around a place I know well from my childhood. When I was younger I often visited with my family, sometimes popping in to see my Grandad Wright's sister, Nellie. She worked at Rowntrees, the chocolate manufacturer. I think she was involved in quality control. Whatever her job was, I remember that when we visited she would always give us bags of misshapen chocolates. Some of them might have looked a bit odd, but they tasted delicious.

These days I don't eat much chocolate, nor do I visit York much. I'm usually too pressed for time. In fact, I nearly had to cancel that day's visit because I'd been called out at 4am to treat an injured alpaca. All I'd been told was that the poor thing had been attacked by a police dog during an operation to tackle a group of car thieves.

Despite the early hour, my mind boggled at the thought of how it had all happened. I'd driven quickly from my home, thinking the animal could be severely injured, its throat ripped to shreds. Luckily, it wasn't. I was pleased to see it had only a little nick by one of its eyes. I was also pleased to hear the police had caught the thieves.

So I did get to York, and strolling through the streets I quickly forgot about animals – but not criminals, because I soon found myself outside the Guy Fawkes pub, very close to York Minster. It was supposedly where the famous gunpowder plotter was born. The notorious Mr Fawkes went to school at St Peter's, a well-known private school in York. Centuries later, my daughter studied there too; I don't suppose she's got much else in common with him. Then I had my first full-on sight of the Minster. Its beauty took my breath away, as it always does. The giant Gothic cathedral is always the centrepiece of any trip to York.

I remembered visiting with my best friend Mark, also a vet, who died in 2009. Lin and I toured the city with him and his wife, Louise. We raced around the Jorvik Centre, which shows the remains of Viking York, and then the railway museum. Somehow we squeezed in a boat trip and afternoon tea – but we still had time for the Minster. As I thought of Mark I couldn't help but feel miserable. He's still sorely missed. Then I suddenly realised, with amazement, that I hadn't been to the Minster since 1995, when I attended Alf's memorial service. It was a huge event for the world's most famous vet, beautifully done, but still upsetting. Even now I can see, in my mind's eye, Jim's pale and drawn face as he paid tribute to his father in front of around 2,000 people.

Luckily, I was pulled back to the present – and happier thoughts – when I stopped to view a temporary stand outside the Minster.

It was more or less a big blackboard on which people were being invited to write with coloured chalks, answering questions such as: when did you feel most alive? I enjoyed reading some of the answers, including one that said, "laughing at small things with loved ones", and another that read simply: "Scarborough, 95-98".

I made my way into the Minster and stood gazing around, immediately having a flashback to climbing thousands of stone steps to its roof when I was about eight. I was wrong, of course. There are only 275 steps. But in the 1960s, it was the highest building I'd ever been in, and it seemed to take forever to climb to the top. It was thrilling to see all the people below scurrying around like ants. I didn't have the time or energy to scale the steps on this trip, though, which was fine, for I was soon having a nice chat with the Reverend Geoffrey Haysmore. He came over to tell me the Minster's huge organ was away being repaired (it will take two years) and that his wife enjoyed The Yorkshire Vet. When I showed Geoffrey a photograph on my phone of his grinning boss, the Archbishop of York, with Jeanie Green in Thirsk, he told me the Archbishop enjoyed the programme too. High praise indeed.

The next stop on my whistle-stop tour of the city was a toy shop I frequented as a small boy, when I was always desperate to buy yet another farm animal or implement. I would invariably get fed up of being dragged around Marks and Spencer and Browns Department Store by my mother and Granny Duncalf, but would try my best not to moan. I knew that if I behaved I would be rewarded with not only fish and chips but a new toy too.

I didn't always get what I wanted though, including a train set I'd set my heart on. At least, not until I was in my 20s and my university girlfriend kindly bought me one. Monk Bar Model Shop seemed to be just how I remembered it all those years ago. I stepped inside and was instantly captivated all over again by farm and agricultural toys made by a firm called Britains. My favourite as a boy was a little elevator used to pick up bales of hay. A man on the till told me another York toy shop I'd often visited in the 1960s, called Precious, was long gone, driven out by competition from far bigger stores. "We've kept going through charm and good luck," he joked, before telling me Britains toys had naturally changed with the times. "I haven't," I replied.

I left the shop and continued my walk around the city centre, soon passing the medieval King's Manor. The red-bricked building is part of the university now, but in the 1630s King Charles I spent some time there. The city effectively became his northern capital while he fought the Scots. He also holed up in York after fleeing London in 1642; it had become too dangerous in the South as support for the Parliamentarians grew. The King's Manor is near some lovely riverside gardens and I recalled that the museum inside them contains a very special hoard. There, in the bowels of the building and not currently on public display, is a collection of more than 1,500 coins buried near Thirsk in the Civil War between Charles' Royalist soldiers and the Parliamentarians, who wanted to oust him. I know a fair bit about the coins because they were discovered by accident in 1985, more than three centuries later, by a farming friend of mine. The hoard is considered one of the most important ever found because of its size, the mix of coins spanning more than a century, and their fantastic condition.

They were stumbled upon by Chris Greensit on his farm at Breckenbrough. Even now he finds the odd ancient coin on his land, but the day he found an entire hoard was undoubtedly a unique one for the bachelor. He's 85 now and has lived his entire life in and around the farmhouse he was born in. The farm is a lush and tranquil spot where Chris has tended his stock, grown crops and, for a time, bred racehorses. He left school at 15 and has never been abroad. He's been to London once, though – for a livestock show. I often visit Chris to attend to his beef cattle. Despite his age, he still has 30 of them on his 170 acres, although he used to have more when he was younger. He gets up at 4.40am every day, even in winter, to keep the farm ticking over, expertly tending his vegetable garden and baling up silage.

On the walls of his old-fashioned kitchen is red distemper, an old type of paint, and there's an armchair at the back for the comfort of his dog, Meg. Chris moves slowly nowadays, but is the perfect host when he's not working. (He runs the farm with the help of a labourer in his early 60s called Brian Robinson. They've worked together for 45 years.) Chris pours out tea for visitors into old blue and white china cups and saucers and offers them scones and butter. His dinner, perhaps a sausage casserole, often simmers away in a slow cooker. He sometimes makes gates and wall decorations from old horseshoes and thinks most of what's on TV is not worth watching, although he has featured on The Yorkshire Vet.

At least he has electricity now. He can still remember life before it, when his family used paraffin lamps and ate pigeons, fresh from the pigeon cote. The rhythm of Chris' life is one that's in keeping with nature, one he's stuck to for years. It probably keeps him going, especially since the death in 2018 of his younger brother Will, also a bachelor, who lived and worked with him. Chris is philosophical about life, sometimes saying: "I'm satisfied with what I've got. Some people never are, no matter what they've got." It could be an attitude influenced by his childhood experiences during the Second

World War. He remembers seeing prisoners of war on the farm, sent from their nearby camp to help out. Chris still has toys and small paintings of sheep made by some of the prisoners, who were no doubt grateful to find safety in Yorkshire.

Chris can easily recall the events of 11 June 1985, when he discovered the coins. It was a Tuesday and he and then 28-year-old Brian were in the foldyard, a covered area used for livestock. Chris has retold the story in his matter-of-fact-manner many times.

"We were levelling t'yard off to cement it out. Then Brian said tractor's shovel 'ad 'it summat."

Chris climbed out of the driver's seat and saw what that something was: a green-glazed ceramic jug, about nine inches down, which had been covered over with a heavy stone. They could both have been covered over with concrete for all eternity that day. Instead, the jug lay broken, presumably damaged by the tractor, with some of its precious contents spilled out into the soil.

I'd like to think that Chris or Brian said, if not thought: "Where there's muck, there's brass," as they began picking up several small, thin and flat pieces of metal. It was money from a very long time ago, something they quickly realised as they stared down at tiny crowned heads next to inscriptions in Latin. Peering in to what was left of the pot, they soon realised they were looking at hundreds and hundreds of coins, in all likelihood not touched by another human being for centuries. There'd been no desert island or rum involved and no "X" to mark the spot, but these two Yorkshiremen had nevertheless found buried treasure. They immediately fetched Chris' brother Will from a nearby field. "By, you'll 'ave 'ell of a job counting all o' them," was his first comment.

There was even more excitement to come in the form of some rolled-up paper the men saw in the pot. "In the sunshine we made out the word 'cheese'," said Chris, "but it wasn't easy to read." The other words were illegible but the old paper, protected by the pot from the elements, would later turn out to be a vital part of the discovery. The farmers then poured their hoard onto their white kitchen table and after counting out more than 1,500 coins (some were stuck together) they were, as Chris said, "a bit foxed" about what to do next. He has some photographs of him and his brother sitting by a pile of coins and bits of the broken pot, a 1985 calendar hanging on the wall nearby. They are both smiling; Will looks chuffed to bits. In one picture you can see the kitchen window behind the brothers and the coins, and a light brown car parked in the farmyard. It's strange to think someone had buried their booty just a few metres from where the farmers were sitting staring at them, back when tractors hadn't even been invented, let alone cars.

Chris knew he couldn't keep the cache just because it had been found on his land. And what would he do with the coins anyway? "They were no good to me," he said. It was up to the authorities to decide who the legal owner was. So Chris telephoned the police in Thirsk, who advised him to contact the coroner. He was told there would have to be an inquest. He placed the coins in a plastic bucket in a shed for safekeeping, a guard dog nearby, before the coins were taken away to be examined by experts. It took weeks, but it was soon clear that the farmers had literally struck gold. Or, to be 100% accurate, 30 gold coins and 1,552 silver ones. The gold was in particularly good condition, showing it had hardly been touched, although much of the silver money was worn, dented and chipped.

Coroners usually deal with inquests into the cause of unusual deaths, but they also have a secondary job dealing with what are known as treasure troves. The Thirsk coroner in 1985 was Peter Hatch, a man renowned for his unstuffy approach and the bow ties he liked to wear. Journalists had learned not to be surprised if he sometimes forgot to turn up at inquests. For this particular case, Mr Hatch, a retired solicitor, had a special request from the man who had found the coins. Chris was concerned the inquest could interfere with harvest time. He asked if it could be delayed. "Don't rush now, we are busy," Chris said. "Put it off a bit." His request was granted.

The discovery had made national headlines and there was intense interest when the inquest finally got underway in Thirsk. It certainly took the farmers, used to getting up early all year round to feed their stock and plough their fields, out of their comfort zone. Chris and Brian arrived early to see several journalists and TV crews outside the courthouse and asked them: "What's on today?" They were told that someone had found some coins. "That was us," Chris replied, and was interviewed again. I wish I'd gone to the inquest. From all accounts, it sounded like a pure piece of theatre. The coins, and to some extent the farmers, were the stars against a backdrop of Civil War turmoil and terror. The inquest heard that the coins were worth about £90 when they had been buried, an incredible amount considering a shepherd in the 1640s might have earned about £5 a year. In 1985, they had a bullion (melting down) value of £1,163, but of course their historical value meant they were worth a lot more than that. They were dated from the 1480s to 1643, and included gold coins minted by Charles I at his mint in York, which he'd brought North because of the fighting.

The coroner said that for reasons of security and convenience it would be photographic evidence, and not the coins themselves, that would be shown to the jury. They heard all about them, though. There were half crowns, shillings, sixpences and more, covering the reigns of various monarchs, but, surprisingly, not Henry VIII. As well as being a terrible husband, his coins were apparently terrible too; their silver wasn't good enough for the job. People just spent them. That left the better coins from other monarchs, including Elizabeth I, to be buried in a hole in what would later be Chris's farm. In all their years underground, the coins were trampled over by hundreds, perhaps thousands, of animal hooves, mere inches away.

The coins were one thing, the pot's brittle paper contents another. The farmers, and everyone else at the inquest, were intrigued to hear about this welcome door onto the past, which helped to give a date for the burial of the hoard. The paper had, amazingly, been preserved by a perfect storm of ingredients: the pot, the right kind of soil conditions (not too wet and not too dry) and a lack of oxygen. Expert analysis found the paper was, in fact, two receipts, for a total of 12 stones of cheese. Sadly, we don't know which kind of cheese, but we do know it was bought in the 1640s by a man called John Guy. He was Deputy Provider General for the Royalist army's York garrison, meaning he sorted out food and drink for the King's soldiers. As well as cheese, he would have probably bought bread and maybe some beef, and of course beer to wash it all down with. The scraps of paper handled with care by my friend's rough and dirty hands were, in essence, 17th-century IOUs promising to pay a farmer or landowners back for the cheese when the king won the war. Whoever had buried these IOUs obviously thought the king would still have been around to pay up after the fighting had ended. How wrong they were.

Of course, we know he didn't win; Charles not only lost the war, he lost his head, executed after the Parliamentarians' victory. But that grisly finale was all to come, and 20th-century experts concluded that whoever was responsible for hiding the money likely got digging in the spring or summer of 1644. The spring was when the Scots arrived in the area to join forces with the Parliamentarians. The summer was when the Battle of Marston Moor took place a few miles from York. The Royalists were heavily defeated, with many fatalities. During those turbulent few months many families might have buried their money, if they had any. They didn't have banks and would have worried that their homes and assets were at risk from marauding armies. As ever, no one knew what the future held.

So who buried the coins? Considering most people back then had very little cash, the money Chris found on his land had to have been buried by someone wealthy enough to have access to such a vast sum, probably a rich landowner. In 1644, the Greensits' farmhouse hadn't yet been built. Instead, there was a small castle called Breckenbrough on the site. It's long gone, apart from a grassy mound near Chris's house. But in 1624 the castle was bought by Sir Arthur Ingram, a well-connected and unpleasant MP, Customs official and wealthy banker with strong links to the king. Charles I is even thought to have stayed with Sir Arthur in his York home for a while. Sir Arthur died in 1642 and was buried at Westminster Abbey, before the hoard was buried. But, of course, his castle, farmland and other assets survived him. It seems most likely that the money came from Sir Arthur's estate, but we will never be certain.

Whoever buried the coins, they no doubt did not imagine they would never be able to reclaim them. It's fascinating to think what might have happened to them. Perhaps they were killed or sent

Peter with Lee and his beloved pet Maisie.

elsewhere in the country. Perhaps a building was knocked down, hiding the burial spot. What we do know is that that the green jug of goodies lay undisturbed for more than three centuries, last touched by an individual worried about the unfolding of the war.

In the end, the jury decided the coins had been deliberately deposited and concealed so therefore they, and the "cheese" papers, were deemed treasure trove and the property of the crown. The jug was not, though, so Chris decided to give it to Sion Hill Hall, an Edwardian stately home near his farm. Its curator had cleaned and identified the coins. The jug was pieced back together and put on display at the hall, while the coins were displayed in York.

Despite not being able to keep the coins, the Greensits did get around £12,000 compensation for their find. Chris had hoped to receive more for the coins, but it was certainly better than nothing. And the men had unearthed some genuine pieces of history. The brothers once went to see the hoard when it was on display at York's Castle Museum. It was a rare trip out for them. When they arrived, a man asked them what they'd come for. "We've come to see the coins," Chris told him. "We aren't going to pay, though; they are our coins." Luckily, the siblings were allowed in for nothing. In the end, seeing the coins displayed didn't make much of an impression. "We'd seen them on the kitchen table for a long while already," said Chris. "They were just the same."

Chris's story was evidence, if any were needed, that York really is the place to see and feel the history of our country. That's why so many people visit, bringing in a more modern kind of coinage that has made the city wealthy. But my next appointment – the real reason I'd come to York in the first place – hammered home that not everyone has financial resources.

As a vet, I see and hear some extraordinary stories about animals – and people. Some stories have a happy ending, some don't. But whatever the outcome of a particular case, I am constantly amazed by the warmth and generosity that flows from the love of animals. Whether it's a farmer who has been up all night to do his utmost to ensure every lamb and mother survives, or a tearful child beside themselves with worry over a poorly pet gerbil, animals can bring out the best in our natures. I see this on an almost daily basis, but just occasionally I come across a case that stands out from the rest, a story that would tug at even the coldest of cold hearts. My meeting with a 42-year-old homeless man called Lee and his lovely old dog Maisie in the shadow of York Minster is one such story. His tale – and the help he has received – shows just how important animals are in the human world.

I found Lee sitting patiently in a doorway in York city centre, snuggled up with Maisie. They were hoping passers-by would give them either food or perhaps some money to buy something to eat. It was immediately apparent that their lives were a world away from mine, not to mention most of the clients I help. They were sitting together on a quaint and charming street called Stonegate. Lee was cross-legged on the concrete amongst the clutter of consumer culture near a restaurant called The York Roast Company. It's well known for selling roast dinners in a Yorkshire pudding wrap. I don't know how Lee can bear to sit near its window full of delicious-looking and aromatic food. When I met him, around mid-afternoon, he said he'd only eaten half a sausage roll that day. I saw straight away that he loved his dog – and the feeling was mutual. Maisie, a 10-year-old Staffordshire bull terrier, was content to sit with her owner. She'd been on Lee's lap as we approached and I'd seen him making a fuss of her. They had a strong bond, I thought.

I was introduced to Lee and Maisie by a bubbly and animal-mad mother-of-four called Fiona Willis. As a child there were tortoises in her family's bathroom. For a while there was even a caged ferret in the downstairs toilet. Now Fiona is a Skeldale client; she shares her Thirsk home with three dogs that I occasionally have to treat. She used to be a vet's receptionist for one of our competitors, but I'll let her off for that because now she spends more than half of her working week volunteering for an animal charity called Street Paws. I'm proud to be one of its patrons. The charity was set up in Newcastle in 2016 by a woman called Michelle Southern. At that time, she was a veterinary practice manager who saw the need for free care for animals owned by homeless and vulnerably housed people. Today Street Paws operates in more than 20 cities and towns across Britain, and sees around 200 animals a month.

Michelle is the charity's full-time – and unpaid – director who oversees about 300 volunteers who are either vets or veterinary nurses. They work in rotas, visiting pets and their owners on the streets or at special sessions at places where homeless people and their dogs gather. They arrange treatment for any animal that needs it. Street Paws has made a big splash; it has even featured on ITV's This Morning. That led to a spike in interest and funding, including a cheque for £1,500 from one particularly impressed viewer. Hearing about all this good work going on, I jumped at the chance to see Street Paws in action when Fiona invited me to York to meet Lee and Maisie.

As Lee and I shook hands on a rainy June day and I bent down to pat Maisie, who was delighted to see Fiona again, I thought, for the umpteenth time, that the Staffordshire Bull Terrier is a breed too often unfairly maligned. My daughter has one called Jake, a lovely animal and best friend to my grandson Archie – they've grown up together. Within a few minutes of talking to Lee, I was also thinking: alter his modern clothes and he could be slap bang in Victorian Britain. What would Charles Dickens, the world-famous writer who railed against poverty, think if he reappeared in the 21st century and learned about the hundreds of homeless people who die in Britain each year?

Lee has had Maisie since she was four months old. Those early days were a very different era, a time of normality when Lee had a job and lived with his girlfriend. "We were well off and had a nice way of life back then," he told me matter-of-factly. He explained how the couple had come to have their pet. It was not a good story. One day they were at home when they heard some horrible noises coming from the flat below. They went downstairs and saw a man basically using Maisie as a punch bag. It turned out he'd broken the puppy's right leg in two places. She also had a broken tail, a couple of broken ribs and some missing teeth. Lee said he had punched the culprit for what he had done to the dog. "I'm not proud of hitting him," he said. "But I don't like seeing animals bashed about." He's a man after my own heart. Lee gave the dog abuser £30 for Maisie, saying it was "the best £30 I ever spent". Lee and his girlfriend then took the frightened puppy into their home, and their hearts, but not before heading straight to a vet to get the dog fixed up. While Maisie was recuperating, they even built her a special step so she could get onto their bed.

I could see the dog had recovered nicely from her horrific beating a decade earlier, and she still had plenty of life in her. Although she was an old lady by the time we met, she was still alert for any sign of trouble. A woman nearby almost jumped out of her skin when Maisie suddenly reared up and barked ferociously at a passing dog. Maisie's intense reaction to a fellow canine merely walking past on a lead wasn't surprising; she's been bitten before. The story then turned to Lee and how his life had taken a turn for the worse. He said he'd been homeless for more than two years and is often hungry and cold, not to mention tired and isolated. He's also very bored. "It drives me crazy," he said. If it wasn't for Maisie and her companionship, he might have given up by now. I'm sure I would have given up already; I'm a pessimist at the best of times.

Lee is a quietly spoken man who still manages to smile. He even laughs. "You have to be positive," he said. "There's no point letting yourself go too much. That's when alcohol and drugs take over." Those twin demons are not something he has given way to at the moment, he said, but he admits he doesn't know what might happen if he has to spend a few more years on the streets. Lee was born in York and moved to Tadcaster when he was seven. He's clearly bright and is keen to get back into work. IT and computers were his passion straight from school. Fixing and reselling them were part of what he did. He was then headhunted, he said, before ending up at Tadcaster's John Smith's brewery. He travelled a lot in those days and earned more than £30,000 a year. Then, about five years ago, he was made redundant. His girlfriend, a highly paid supermarket manager who was frequently parachuted into problem stores, took redundancy with him so they could pool their money and invest in property development. With Maisie, they moved to Hartlepool, where they had great success with the first two houses they bought, did up and sold. "We felt like professionals," said Lee. But property number three led them onto the streets.

Have you seen the 1998 film *Sliding Doors*, starring Gywneth Paltrow? The movie shows her character living two parallel lives. One life is based on what happens after she just manages to catch a particular tube train in London. The other life is based on what happens if she misses the train. She's the same person, but the viewer sees two very different lives with two very different endings. For Lee, the moment he saw a house "from the kerbside", before purchasing it at auction without his girlfriend being there, was surely his *Sliding Doors* event. "Had she gone too, we wouldn't have bought it," he said. The purchase turned out to be a disaster. It bankrupted the couple. Lee laughed with what seemed to be genuine humour when he explained that the bailiffs had been kind enough to drop them all off in York with their remaining possessions. The three were left in a small park near the train station. There, each day, "a bit more of our stuff would disappear. We couldn't protect it 24 hours a day."

Lee and his girlfriend were still together when I met Lee, and he said she had just been given a one-bedroomed flat. He was allowed to stay there three nights a week. It was all the rules would allow until her tenancy became permanent. She had to prove she was a good tenant first, said Lee, and then he could move in with her. "They don't want people letting all their friends in to doss down or maybe turn the place into a drug den or party house." So for the time being Lee was still spending a lot of time on the streets with Maisie, often sleeping in a tent in a green area well away from the city centre. They slept there to try to avoid those who might hassle them – sometimes other homeless people, sometimes drunks on a Saturday night out. Occasionally, there were people intent on stealing Maisie, and Lee has faced violence on the streets, but having a dog can often serve as protection. Maisie usually scared attackers off, he said, and because Lee knew she was by his side and would bark at strangers, he could relax a bit more and get some sleep. To me, it sounded like having to navigate a minefield while blindfolded.

Lee and his girlfriend tended to live on fast food and sandwiches that they were given or managed to buy. Sometimes they had no money to eat. Maisie ate better than they did, as people would often donate dog food; Lee said he gave some away when he got too much. "She never goes without," he said. "There's never been a day when she's not eaten. She comes first. People often think you have a dog on the streets just to get money, but it's not like that." Having a dog can actually make life more difficult for Lee. It's not easy to get accommodation partly because of Maisie, he told me. "I've been offered places, but the landlord won't take her. I'd never give her up, though." Some hostels won't take dogs either, one of the things Street Paws is working hard to address. One recent success came with a Manchester charity called SPIN that works with the homeless. Street Paws paid for it to have two custom-built kennels, so people on the streets can turn up and stay, with their dogs in tow. Street Paws was also pleased Rotherham Council now has some emergency accommodation for homeless people with dogs. It hopes more local authorities will follow suit.

Although Lee was living outside more than he might need to because he refused to get rid of Maisie, I didn't blame him for hanging on to her for dear life. More people stop for a chat with homeless people when there's a dog involved; we all need human interaction. Plus, there's a mountain of evidence showing people's mental health improves when they are around animals. That's why there are, for example, organisations like one called Therapy Dogs that take dogs into hospitals and old people's homes. Dogs can help with things like stress, anxiety and depression. Maisie has certainly been good for Lee.

Street Paws volunteers have been receiving mental health training so they can cope better with the upsetting things they see and hear. When I met Lee in York, he was trying to mentally prepare himself for an upsetting event that at that point was probably not too far in the future: the death of Maisie. Street Paws was able to introduce me to Lee because it had got to know him through treating his dog – her kidneys were failing. Lee had first realised something was wrong when Maisie started vomiting and losing weight. "You could see her spine not long ago," said Lee. Just before Street Paws got involved, he was advised to have Maisie put to sleep. Thank goodness for Fiona, who saw just how important Maisie was to Lee. She arranged for volunteer vets from Vets4Pets (in York, Street Paws also works with the Minster Veterinary Practice) to do some tests on Maisie for a detailed diagnosis. They then prescribed medication and a special diet suited to her condition. Because of Street Paws, Lee didn't pay a penny.

Four months on, when I met Maisie, she was eating properly again and had gained weight. She was perky and interested. "She's almost back to her former self," said Lee. She'd been given some extra, quality time with her owner. Lee was hoping for a few more months with her and said he wouldn't get another dog after she died, at least, not until his own life was back on track. I felt quite emotional and wanted to hug Lee, Maisie and Fiona in the doorway, but instead I disappeared for a few minutes. I'd decided to arrange for a few hot meals for him. I'm sorry to report that two places turned me down when I explained I wanted to buy some hot food in advance for Lee. My idea was to get the restaurant to give me a receipt showing how much I had paid so he could redeem it when he was hungry. The third place I tried, though, did me proud. It's called Middle Feast and is on Lendal. If you go to York, do pop in; it's good cooking.

You could have also given your regards to Lee and Maisie, but sadly only one of them is around now. Maisie went downhill not long after we met and had to be put to sleep. Lee was, of course, devastated. I'm hoping that by the time you read this, he will at least have a permanent roof over his head. I'm also hoping he'll be able to get another dog in the not too distant future. Then, they can snuggle up together on the sofa, not in a doorway. That's surely not too much to ask.

CHAPTER 12

The Remains of
Oliver Cromwell

One of the lovely things about dealing with animals is that they do bring a certain simplicity to life. When a creature is sick or injured, I try to make it better again. It doesn't matter whether it's a treasured pet or a cow working for its keep, my job is to do my best to make each animal fit and healthy. And it's of no concern to me who owns that injured or sick patient. In the 38 years I've been a vet I've called on all kinds of people – rich and poor, from right across the social spectrum – to hopefully allay their fears by successfully treating their animals. These thoughts crossed my mind recently as I was driving past Newburgh Priory, a country estate near Thirsk that's been in the hands of the same family for centuries. The family's ancestors might contain more than a smattering of lords and ladies, but they are the same as everyone else when it comes to a sick animal: they just want their loved one put right as quickly as possible.

My first recollection of going to the Priory must have been 30 or so years ago when the cat got among the pigeons, so to speak. The cat had actually managed to catch the family's canary, not a pigeon, but you know what I mean. Somehow or other the bird survived and I was called in to treat it, although having looked after tens of thousands of animals in my time I must admit that my memories of the incident are a bit hazy. The canary was shocked but in pretty good shape; the only real problem was that its feathers didn't grow back. But I usually find there's a solution to most problems and this one was no different.

The grandma of the child who owned the bird stepped into the breach and knitted the little thing a woollen jumper to cover its bald patches. It was a lovely gesture, even though, considering the size of a canary, it probably didn't take too long to make. Another case involving the same family, also many years ago, concerned a hamster with a prolapsed uterus. The little girl who looked after her adored her pet. She was inconsolable at the sight of the poorly creature. Prolapsed uteruses in small animals are notoriously difficult to deal with, and they often die of shock before or during the operation. Thankfully, I managed to put the hamster right, and she survived the surgery to spin on her wheel once more.

Much more recently, I also treated a donkey at the estate that had to be castrated. It was an incident that I remember very clearly, having gone along with my colleague Sarah Beckerlegge. Brought up in America listening to Herriot audio books and watching *All Creatures Great and Small*, Sarah was a mere toddler, probably about three years old, when she told her Yorkshire mum that she wanted to be a vet like James Herriot. Her mother is very proud that Sarah grew up to fulfil her dream when she became an equine expert and later got a job at Skeldale, with its links to Alf Wight. I'm just glad to have someone around who probably knows more about donkeys and horses than I do. On the day in question, Sarah was heavily pregnant, so needed to be kept well out of harm's way during the donkey's castration. She came along, but I had to do the operation. That's how I found myself on a gloomy February day dealing with the business side of the transaction. In a stable with very little light, Sarah anaesthetised the donkey and we gently laid him down. It was a cold day and my fingers were freezing; I was having trouble getting them moving. But what I saw next stopped me in my tracks. "Bloody hell! Those are the biggest testicles I've ever seen on a donkey!" I exclaimed. Perhaps the animal heard me and was offended; he tensed up then half-heartedly twitched a few times, despite being fully unconscious. I took them off, but the size of those awesome things will live long in my memory.

The same family at the Priory have asked for Skeldale's help on many occasions and I'm glad to say that there have been a number of successes along the way, involving several much-loved animals. Sarah once went out in the middle of a winter's night to help a black and white miniature Shetland pony on the estate. Domino, as she was called, would often pull children around in a little cart, but on this particular night the poor little mite, who stood not much higher than Sarah's knees, couldn't even walk, let alone trot. She was laying on her back in an old barn with her legs in the air and looked at death's door. She had a bad case of colic, which is a severe abdominal pain. It might sound like nothing to worry about, but it can be fatal. Sarah couldn't manage to feel inside Domino because she was so tiny, so she ran a tube through her nose and into her stomach, to find out if there was any fluid in there that shouldn't be. Luckily there was none, so the pony simply received an injection to ease the pain. Within a few minutes she was up and eating, and in less than an hour she was trying to escape from the barn. It wasn't long before Domino was pulling the laughing children around again in the cart.

Of course, it hasn't always gone well for the family's animals. That's life, but it's never easy for the owner – or the vet. The family once had a lovely young labrador called Oscar who had a nasty inflammation in his bones. Treatment seemed to be helping him, when he suddenly had a stroke and died before we could do anything. It was just awful. "Another old mate gone," I always think. More recently, a black Labrador called Widget became poorly with progressive anaemia, which is sometimes a sign of a blood cancer. He had to be put to sleep. It's funny how the sad times stay with vets more than the successes.

Owners, though, certainly remember the happy times. They love their pets. Every day, I see how much joy animals bring to their human companions. A recent survey found that in Britain there are about 11 million pet cats and nine million pet dogs. That's about one cat or dog for every three humans – an enormous figure. These numbers show that age, social background and political views are irrelevant when it comes to caring for our furry friends. Everyone, including those at the higher echelons of society, can crumple when faced with a sick animal. Widget the black labrador, the sweater-wearing canary, the hamster with the problematic uterus, the donkey with larger-than-life testicles and the pony suffering from colic: we love them all.

It's strange how a single glimpse of a house can set in motion a train of thought. I should say, of course, that Newburgh Priory is not any ordinary house. The home – and the animals I've just described – belong to the aristocratic Wombwell family. They're like any other animal lovers: upset and on tenterhooks when their pets are poorly, beaming and over the moon when they recover. They live a few miles from me in one of the most alluring houses I have ever seen. Their home is a reminder of another of the great attractions of Yorkshire: its wealth of fabulous stately homes.

Newburgh Priory is on the edge of the Howardian Hills, near the village of Coxwold. The house is a mere fraction of the magnitude of Castle Howard, 15 miles away, which really was built to impress. But Newburgh's smaller size is part of its immeasurable charm, and it's still extremely impressive. Driving through its gates onto a gravel drive is to enter another time, almost another dimension. The sight of the topiary is an enjoyable prelude to 40 acres of landscaped gardens and grounds that have magnificent lawns, hidden gardens and woodland walks. There's even an oak tree planted by Queen Victoria's grandson Prince Albert Victor, on his "first visit" to the home. Gaze past the swans on the lake and you can see the White Horse of Kilburn in the distance.

The gardens perfectly offset the mellowed stone house, also a wondrous sight to behold. It was built in the 1500s on the site of a 12th-century Augustinian Priory, using the priory's stone. The priory itself had been ransacked when Henry VIII decided to get rid of our monasteries; all that's left of it now are some tiny floor bricks by a tearoom, and the word "priory" in the name of the estate.

The house we see today has been home to the Wombwells and their ancestors for almost five centuries. Although my background is very different to theirs – I grew up on a farm and, to the best of my knowledge, no member of the Royal family has ever stayed in my home – our paths have often overlapped in the course of my work. The Kirkgate vets, then the Skeldale vets, have looked after the Priory's animals for years.

Stephen Wombwell is the current boss at Newburgh, a business-savvy chartered surveyor and genial chap in his early 40s. Apart from stints away for school, university and work, he's lived at the Priory since he was seven years old, and has been there full time since 2010. His parents live in a house on the estate, while he shares the Priory with his partner and the five children they have between them. This phenomenal family home, overflowing with ambience and heirlooms, is certainly big enough for them all, and beautiful enough for anyone. But that's not to say the house and estate are easy to run. There's a great deal to oversee, with about 6,000 acres in all; three-quarters of it is farmland, the rest is woodland. Like all our great country estates, this one has many small farms, which are rented out to tenants. Stephen lets out other properties on his land too, including cottages and pubs. The family also help finance the upkeep of their home by allowing visitors to come in and look round for part of the year.

If that all sounds like a lot of money coming in, it's only fair to say that the grandeur, beauty and history of the Wombwells' house doesn't come cheap. "Not a week goes by without something fundamental breaking," said Stephen, "perhaps the heating, plumbing or electricity." Something went wrong with the boiler a few months ago and the whole system needed replacing, he said, at a cost of £50,000. "I spend £1,000 on lightbulbs a year," he added. Stephen was sitting in the tearoom after dealing with tourists all afternoon, helping his daughter with her homework. "Heating oil costs thousands, and we don't even heat most of the place," he went on. "And the cost of electricity is outrageous. Home insurance is about £20,000. Actually, it's a bargain considering what it is we're insuring!" And there was me thinking my life was stressful. Living the so-called high life at

Newburgh Priory isn't all rosy. As with most things, there are pros and cons. "As long as the pros outweigh the cons – great," said Stephen. "But the second it becomes a nightmare, there's no point." Houses like Newburgh are only worth fighting for if their owners enjoy them, he added. "If not, what is the point? They become a millstone."

The Wombwells seem to have avoided the millstone effect by moving with the times and being creative with how the estate earns extra money. "I will do anything if someone is willing to pay me – within reason," Stephen said with a grin. From plant fairs and Christmas tree sales to car rallies and weddings (the Priory has been a wedding venue for more than 30 years), there's a lot happening. The estate also earns money from pheasant, partridge and duck shoots, and is occasionally used for film and TV shoots. A 2010 drama about 19th-century lesbian aristocrat Anne Lister (the subject of a recent BBC series) was partly shot at Newburgh.

The house also featured in a Robinson Crusoe film. "That was a strange phone call," said Stephen. Quite naturally, he couldn't understand why a tale involving a man shipwrecked on a desert island needed to use the landlocked Priory for any of its scenes. It turned out that the film crew wanted to shoot flashbacks to the hero's life. What's a more impressive claim to fame, though, is the appearance of Stephen and his home in a 2002 film called *Possession*, which featured the star Gwyneth Paltrow. Gentleman that he is, Stephen wouldn't be drawn on any gossip about the actress, apart from giving a glimpse of the less appealing side of filming. "She was bored," he said. "The actors get bored with the daily grind. I was an extra. On screen for just three seconds, but I was hanging around all day for it."

Newburgh Priory, beautifully rebuilt in the 16th century on the site of the old Augustinian Priory.

The Priory doesn't have any extra attractions – like a shop or adventure playground – to bring in tourists, but in my view that's even more of a reason to visit. Sometimes the man of the house himself takes visitors around on a guided tour but he pops up here, there and everywhere, preparing the tearoom or showing visitors where to walk and park. One Wombwell family motto is "In Well Beware". In other words, when things are going well, don't be complacent. Another motto, in French, is "Bonne et Belle Assez" – to be good and beautiful is enough. I can't help but think a more fitting phrase for the Wombwells in the 21st century would be "All hands on deck". After waving yet another car into the correct parking spot on an April day this year, Stephen immediately dashed inside to take the ticket money from a couple of tourists. Then he joked: "That's my evil twin outside. Don't listen to him; he tells all sorts of fibs."

Newburgh is the sort of place that has so much history it makes your eyes water. The cast of characters associated with the estate range from merely interesting to spellbinding. At some point during the Dissolution of the Monasteries, Henry VIII sold Newburgh to one of his chaplains, Anthony de Bellasis, for £1,062 – a massive amount back then, of course. Anthony's nephew William (Stephen's related to both men, I think, but I still can't work out exactly how) created the mansion we see today. Much of it is similar to how it was in Tudor times, while the rest was remodelled in the 1700s.

On a tour of the house you can walk from one century to another, your every move followed by the eyes of the many painted family figures staring down from the walls, among them a pregnant woman, a woman with a missing finger, and two sisters who became nuns. You can meander from dark, ram-packed chambers full of centuries-old chairs, chests and bible boxes, to much brighter stair-ways and rooms with newer Venetian "arm" lamps, ornate mirrors and miniature statues.

You can also pass through an area still damaged by fire, the renovations unfinished because of a "curse" in Georgian times. It's said the son of the house could have saved a maid from being fatally burned, but chose not to, so she cursed the room while she lay dying. If the owner of the house should ever try to finish it, she supposedly said, his son and heir would die an untimely death. Stephen will not touch the room, even though he only has daughters. "I am not running the risk on that technicality," he said.

This is all intriguing stuff, but the house's most interesting story concerns the body of Oliver Cromwell. As we all know, Cromwell was a key Parliamentarian involved in the overthrow and execution of King Charles I in the Civil War. He led the country for five years and was in charge when he died from natural causes in 1658. He was buried in an elaborate state funeral at Westminster Abbey in London, but that's not, apparently, where his body ended up.

About a year before Cromwell's death, Mary, one of his daughters (he had nine children in total) married a skilled political operator whose family owned Newburgh Priory. His name was Thomas Belasyse, or Bellasis, as it has sometimes been written. The family of Mary's new husband had supported Charles I during the Civil War, but Thomas had thrown his weight behind the Parliamentarians, an alliance cemented with his marriage to Cromwell's daughter. The marriage would have allowed him to ingratiate himself with the new Republican regime at a time when his family's sympathics might have been the subject of suspicion. To show just how quickly events can change, though, Thomas changed tack when the monarchy was restored a few years later, finding favour with Charles II, the son of the executed king. As Stephen said of this particular ancestor: "Thomas survived a time he probably shouldn't have done. If he hadn't been as politically astute, the history of Newburgh could have been very different. He could have had everything confiscated and taken away." Instead, Thomas was savvy enough – and lucky enough – to do well under the royals. Later on, he was even made an ambassador in Venice.

Oliver Cromwell's body, or what was left of it, didn't fare nearly as well as his son-in-law's career. What happened to it was well beyond grotesque. The new king's supporters, still smarting about the overthrowing of the monarchy and the beheading of Charles I, dug up Cromwell and two other key Parliamentarians in 1661. The bodies were dragged across London, then hanged at Tyburn (near to today's Marble Arch) before their long-dead heads were placed on 20-foot spikes at Westminster. The remains of the remains were buried in a shallow grave near the gallows. Or were they?

This is the point at which Newburgh Priory – or rather Mary – comes into the tale. It's claimed that she arranged for the headless corpse of her father to be secretly taken from London, after bribing some guards to substitute his body for another. Cromwell's remains went firstly to Northborough Manor near Peterborough, where her late sister had lived. From there, the body allegedly travelled to North Yorkshire and Newburgh Priory. Remember there were no lorries or trains back then; it must have gone, if it did go, by horse and cart. Once at Newburgh, the body was, in theory at least, carried up the old home's creaky stairs and hidden in the roof space. The roof was renovated several decades later by enthusiastic Georgian architects, but the body is said to still be up there.

Visitors to the priory today can stand in a small bare attic space near a cabinet holding a saddle, bridle and pistols. They belonged to a nobleman who, ironically, given what else is said to be in the room, fought for the Royalists against Cromwell's troops. But you hardly notice them as your attention is focused on a bricked up area at the other end of the room. Attached to it is a death mask and a small sign that says: "In this vault it is believed are Oliver Cromwell's bones, brought here by his daughter Mary, Countess of Fauconberg, at the restoration, when his remains were disinterred from Westminster Abbey."

Is the body really there? We all know fact can be stranger than fiction, and I have to say it sounds weirdly possible. Mary and Thomas both had contacts and money to get the job done; on a wall at the Priory is a seven-foot-tall portrait of her wearing a pearl necklace and a red, white and gold gown. Lavish jewellery, clothes and paintings were not for the masses; they didn't come cheap. Mary was also said to have adored her father, so the motivation was certainly there. Perhaps you and I would have tried to do the same in her situation. But how would Mary have persuaded her husband to help? Perhaps, as they chatted over roast venison or strolled arm in arm on the lawn, past a pair of swans, he said: "No! Over my dead body!" – and then had to be persuaded in a week long, room-to-room argument. Or maybe Mary cleverly let him win at backgammon with a few glasses of wine thrown in for good measure, before turning the conversation back to her dead father.

Frustratingly for some, the tomb has never been opened to prove or disprove the Cromwell story. Some experts say it's likely the body remained in a pit in London and is now covered over by concrete, traffic and shoppers. Whatever the truth is, I can understand why the Wombwells continue to keep a lid on the whole thing; the tale of the headless Cromwell keeps everyone guessing. Even the royal family has succumbed to the gory horror of it all, with some of its members itching to know for sure whether the republican leader really is there. Some of them might have seriously wondered what would have happened to the monarchy, and themselves, if he hadn't died when he did; they could have been looking for regular work with the rest of us.

Queen Mary, the wife of King George V and the grandmother of our current Queen, was one blue-blooded visitor who demanded to have the tomb opened. "The family said no, so she went to the Archbishop of Canterbury and told him to make them open it up," said Stephen. "He told her not to be silly. She threw a paddy and said she'd never visit again." That was a huge relief, he added, as she was renowned for stealing things from the many houses she visited. "She thought she could take things. She would extravagantly praise something she liked until people felt they had to give it to her. There were rumours that if you didn't take the hint and offer the item, she would send the butler in to take it anyway." It's been said that after Queen Mary's death in 1953 there was an "amnesty" when the owners of Britain's stately homes could reclaim what was rightfully theirs.

Edward VII was another royal who visited Newburgh and was seemingly obsessed with Cromwell's remains. He was still the Prince of Wales at the time and must have found the historical saga irresistible; he certainly went to great lengths to crack the mystery. He was probably staying at the house while heading north; royals like him "tended to tour round and put up wherever they felt like", Stephen said. Perhaps Edward was bored with the same old fancy dinners and the odd game of croquet. Whatever it was, his interest in the Cromwell story soon turned to desperation. He became determined to crack the tomb open and see with his own eyes if a body was there or not. His partner in crime was a worker from the estate, who, it seems, was bribed by the Prince. The workman would have had both the skills and the tools to carry out the task. It's hard to picture the Prince beavering away with a chisel on his own in the middle of the night. Unfortunately, or fortunately depending on your point of view, it didn't end well. "They nearly got away with it, but the two of them were caught at the tomb in the early hours," said Stephen.

Some say it was the Priory's head gardener who caught them. Others say it was the Lord of the Manor himself, at that time Sir George Orby Wombwell. At just under five feet tall, he was a forceful character who'd had some hair-raising wartime experiences. Clearly, dealing with a naughty Prince just a few years younger than himself was child's play. Edward was thrown out of the Priory soon afterwards (oh, to have witnessed that episode) and was probably disappointed at not getting into the tomb or to the bottom of the Cromwell legend. We can only assume becoming King later on took the edge off any lingering distress. As for the workman, we don't know his name. "Our records are sketchy," said Stephen. "But we know he lost his job." I just hope the bribe was a big one.

There's a gigantic portrait on the Priory's dining room wall of a young Sir George, small, smart and serious in his military uniform with his favourite horse, called The Turk, towering above him. They'd both travelled out to take part in the Crimean War in the 1850s when Sir George was in his early 20s. The soldier and his horse were due to participate in one of the most infamous episodes in British military history, but The Turk was lame on the day of what subsequently became known as the Charge of the Light Brigade, so he didn't. Sir George was not so lucky, and rode into battle on another horse.

He wasn't one of the 100 or so British cavalrymen killed in that suicidal charge against the Russian army, although he did have a horse shot from under him before being captured. Through skill and/ or luck, he somehow managed to escape, in part, apparently, because a detachment of British riders suddenly appeared. Sir George is said to have heard the voice of his commanding officer shout out: "Catch a horse, you young fool, and come with us!" He managed to grab an animal, threw himself on it, and escaped. Dodging bullets, the young man galloped to safety, away from the "jaws of death" and the "mouth of hell" that Lord Tennyson would soon mention in his famous poem about that terrible military disaster.

Sir George and The Turk both returned to Yorkshire, where the horse died at the grand old age of 26. Three of his hooves were, rather gruesomely, made into inkpots and can still be seen today in a cabinet in the study at the house. I suppose this was a sign of affection back then. What remained of The Turk was buried opposite the estate's main gates; a headstone commemorating the famous horse is in the estate grounds.

Sir George had another lucky escape. He managed to survive a tragic ferry accident while out hunting. A dozen men and horses were crossing the swollen River Ure by ferry to chase a fox when their boat capsized. Six men, including a champion swimmer, and nine horses died. It was a huge national story. *The Times* newspaper even said: "The news of the accident has been received throughout the kingdom with as cordial a sorrow as if the catastrophe had been of universal public concern." Tens of thousands lined the funeral route of one of the men. Sir George was not always lucky, though, and his later life was marred by tragedy. His two sons died while on active service overseas, news of the first death in 1889 reaching Yorkshire not long after their father had begun work on the unfinished "cursed" room. No wonder Stephen isn't keen to touch it even now.

Like all of Yorkshire's country homes, Newburgh Priory has a very attractive bounty of history and characters, objects and stories that draw in many tourists. But it's the Cromwell story that really grabs the attention. He still has an impact on the estate almost four centuries after his death. An Irish couple almost cancelled their wedding there at the last minute when they heard about Cromwell's body. "They'd been weaned on stories of him being a bogeyman," said Stephen. I suppose they had a point: Cromwell acted brutally in Ireland when his troops crossed the sea to retake the island. They killed thousands of people. Some visitors, though, specifically seek out Newburgh because of the 'body'. One middle-aged man on a recent tour said he'd visited the house 40 years before and was back purely because of the Cromwell connection. "He's his hero," said his wife.

When the man finally stood next to the attic "tomb", he told their small tour group he had already visited the spot where Cromwell's head resides. As I mentioned earlier, the head had been detached from its body and put on a spike. After being dipped in tar and displayed high above the ground for more than 20 years, it fell to the ground in a storm, so the story goes. A soldier supposedly found it and hid it up his chimney, then bequeathed it to his daughter on his deathbed. The skull is thought to have appeared in a freak show and was sold or passed on several times more, before eventually ending up in the hands of a 20th-century cleric called

Canon Wilkinson. Some say he kept it, protected by glass, on his sideboard. Tests were done in the 1930s and experts said it was likely to be Cromwell's. Whoever it had originally belonged to, it was finally given to Cambridge University in 1960, where both Canon Wilkinson and Cromwell had studied. The skull finally had a dignified burial there.

Nowadays, Stephen's children and their friends like to dress up for Halloween and run around the house, pausing by the tomb to scare themselves silly and take photos. Old boys who studied at Newburgh – it was a school in the 1940s before yet another fire caused a lot of damage – visit occasionally and have said some pupils dared to sleep on top of "Cromwell". One insisted he slept on it alone. Stephen said he himself believes Cromwell's remains are in the rafters of his home, but can't prove it. "You'd have to exhume, which is complicated. And Cromwell is, fundamentally, family through marriage. It's a bit macabre digging up your ancestors for no particular reason. I don't think it would answer the question; there would be all sorts of testing and all the rest of it. The story is probably better than the reality." I'm not the only one who'd love to know, though. Perhaps one day Stephen will change his mind about opening the tomb up. I've got my hammer and chisel at the ready if he needs a hand.

CHAPTER 13

Bernie, Bernie, Show Us Your ****!

've always tried to make time for the "beautiful game" and my team, Middlesbrough, or "Boro", as they are known. But country vets are a busy lot and I have to work many Saturdays – match day. So although the Riverside Stadium is only about 30 miles from my home, it sometimes feels as though it might as well be 500. Work, family life and filming more often than not put paid to my desire to watch a match and escape, even for just a few hours, from the pressures of everyday life. That said, football will always be one of my greatest passions. Whether playing in my younger years or watching in person or at home on the settee, the sport has brought me endless hours of drama, fun and camaraderie. And, of course, angst: it couldn't be anything else when you are a Middlesbrough fan.

Occasionally though, I do manage to wangle a few hours off Skeldale's on-call rota, as I did a little while ago. With a pocket of free time, it wasn't long before I was on my way to Middlesbrough with an old mate to watch them play Norwich City. I was being sensible and keeping my expectations low; I didn't for a second expect the result to go our way. But I knew it would be a welcome break to spend a few hours in the company of my effervescent friend, former Boro player and football commentator Bernie Slaven.

I know the club and the town well. I've been visiting the Riverside and the previous stadium, Ayresome Park, for decades with friends and family, including my grandson, Archie. He was six when I took him to his first game four years ago. I was worried he'd be bored but he was glued to it. It was me who wanted to leave having watched a boring 0-0 draw. Whether you're a regular visitor or an occasional fan, driving into Middlesbrough always reminds you exactly what kind of place it is. The short journey from my home takes me alongside the natural beauty of the Yorkshire Moors. But in no time at all the hills, fields and sheep suddenly give way to a bleak industrial landscape. At least the pollution is significantly less these days.

It's incredible to believe looking at it now that little more than a couple of hundred years ago Middlesbrough was just a farm with about 25 inhabitants. Through the 19th century it industrialised rapidly, and was known for coal, iron and steel, and chemicals. The Transporter Bridge, which is less than a mile from where Boro play, is a vivid reminder of that past. Seeing it in the distance is when the excitement about the approaching game really kicks in. The bridge is unusual in that it transports vehicles across the River Tees in a kind of gondola that takes 90 seconds from one side to the other. It's been in operation since 1911, and is apparently the longest-working bridge of its kind in the world. Mind you, that was still 35 years after my beloved football club opened its doors. The bridge is a local landmark, and even featured in the Oscar-nominated film about a young dancer called Billy Elliot. As well as being an occasional dance venue, it's often used by daredevil abseilers and bungee jumpers. Call me a coward, but I prefer to use the Transporter, as it's known to locals, just to get across the river.

As I drove towards the stadium, I took in some more of the town's industrial landscape. Some people find it unattractive, but I like the in-your-face evidence of history; Middlesbrough's heart worn firmly on its sleeve is part of its considerable charm. Perhaps the town's most important claim to fame is that the world-famous explorer, Captain James Cook, was born in a nearby village. But, as inspiring as he was, the workers who built the products that travelled the world are my real heroes.

It was Middlesbrough that provided the materials for Sydney's Harbour Bridge in the 1920s and 30s. The town was so important to Britain's economy that the Germans bombed it to hell in the war. It was actually the first major British settlement to be targeted by the Luftwaffe; the Blitz certainly wasn't just in London. Today much of Middlesbrough's old heavy industry is gone, although some remains. There's thankfully still a thriving port and chemical sector, as well as newer industries; would you believe the town is now a go-to place for digital animation?

Then there are the people. Sister Ann Lilly, an elderly nurse I knew from nearby Stockton, would have been proud of Middlesbrough's ability to adapt, I thought, as the football stadium loomed large in front of me. She herself certainly did a good job of moving with the times. Sister Lilly – that's what we vets always called her – was one of the very first radiographers in Britain, when little was known about X-rays. She'd sometimes give our veterinary practice in Thirsk old but still-working hospital equipment from Middlesbrough or Northallerton, including a proper machine to sterilise our instruments.

We were mainly acquainted with Sister Lilly, though, because of her unwavering dedication to animals. For decades she rescued and rehomed huge numbers of abandoned cats and dogs. Her character is known to millions because Alf wrote about her, changing her name to "Sister Rose" in his Herriot books. In 2013, aged 100 and only a few months before she died, Sister Lilly was among a handful of people honoured at a prestigious awards ceremony for their work with animals. She received a lifetime achievement award and had a wonderful time in London, even meeting rock star Brian May from Queen. She later told a friend: "An old man with long grey hair kept coming up to me and asking if I was alright." She had no idea Brian was one of the most famous guitarists in the world. At any rate, I'm sure he knew who the true celebrity of the night was.

I was soon turning into the stadium's busy car park. I pulled over and, surrounded by noisy football fans every which way, I decided to stretch my legs and have a quick look at the statues of Boro and England legends Wilf Mannion and George Hardwick, just in front of the ground. I grinned as I recalled an afternoon, many years ago, back at the old stadium, when I'd had the pleasure of bumping into Wilf. He was known as the Golden Boy and was one of the best-ever Boro players, as well as proudly taking the field for his country on more than 20 occasions. Bernie Slaven once told me that when Wilf signed something, he'd often add the words: Boro, England, Great Britain. He was a pensioner in his 70s on the day I met him. I didn't know Wilf personally, but when I saw him in the toilets at halftime I instantly recognised him. Middlesbrough weren't doing too well at all; we were already three-nil down, so it's not surprising the words just popped out of my mouth. "Get your boots back on Wilf, we need you!"

Bernie Slaven in a 3-3
draw with Sheffield
United Division
Two league match
at Ayresome Park,
Saturday 2 September
1989.

I like to watch matches from the stands, just like everyone else, but on my day out with Bernie I was going as a VIP, and so made my way to a reception area at the front of the stadium. I immediately caught sight of Bernie's smart suit and tie as he stood waiting, chatting to someone who wanted to talk to him, as they always do. They were taking a selfie as I walked up. I'm used to seeing that happen; Bernie's a popular man and although he retired from playing football in 1995, he still gets approached regularly by fans, particularly in Middlesbrough. The crowd at Ayresome Park would often chant his name: "Bernie Bernie Slaven, Bernie Bernie Slaven", and although he didn't join the Boro until he was 24, he still managed to play 382 games and score an awe-inspiring 147 goals.

Later on, Bernie carved out a second career as a commentator, for which his quick brain and high-speed conversation is perfectly suited. He commentated for years with the late, great radio broadcaster Ali Brownlee (known as the Voice of the Boro) on hundreds of Middlesbrough games. They were a massively popular and award-winning double act with a fantastic rapport. Ali was optimistic and cheerful about the team, while Bernie was much more critical and, dare I say, more realistic. On one occasion he was so exasperated by Boro's performance, he threw his headphones down in a paddy and stormed off, live on air.

I knew of Bernie long before he knew of me. He was, after all, a star player for my team; I'd seen him in action countless times. He used to live in a village near me, so when I saw him building a wall in his garden 15 years ago I stopped my car and went to introduce myself over his hedge. It was the perfect opportunity to meet one of my heroes, although by this time he had retired. We found out that we had more in common than football. Bernie loves animals and over the years has shared his home with many different kinds, from cats and dogs to goats and peacocks. We were soon firm friends and I became his vet, which sometimes meant I had to take hard decisions.

I remember once Bernie was away in London playing five-a-side football and his father was looking after his animals for a few days. Unfortunately, the old man gave too many apples to one of Bernie's ponies, which then developed colic. I couldn't save him and he had to be put to sleep before Bernie returned home. He was naturally upset, but didn't hold it against me or his dad.

Some years later Bernie moved away; he now lives in a village closer to Middlesbrough so I'm no longer his vet, but I still try to keep up with his animals' antics. Most recently, he has had more traditional pets, including two gorgeous Irish Setters, sisters called Carrot and Cinnamon. He loves walking with them in the hills, often taking photographs of spectacular sunsets along the way.

Bernie is not embarrassed about his love of animals: I've heard him talk very fondly about a blackbird called Betty. It gives him great pleasure to see her enjoying his garden. Over the years our friendship has developed to such an extent that we did a half marathon together in New York. And I really enjoy watching football with him, given the chance.

After meeting in reception, we walked up a flight of stairs before making our way down various corridors towards a "backstage" area. As we went, our conversation was interrupted every few metres by people who either knew Bernie or wanted to know him. As I watched, I thought about how he'd once told me he'd have been a joiner if he hadn't had a knack for scoring goals. The world of football would have been a far less interesting place if he had picked up a piece of wood. But he is also a decent man with solid principles. He does a lot to help people in need, often getting involved with charity work. As we walked down yet another corridor, I remembered the tweet (he has 30,000 followers) he'd sent out a couple of days beforehand about homelessness. A television programme on the issue had upset Bernie so much that he'd gone online and offered to help with projects to tackle homelessness on Teesside. His love for mankind runs parallel to his love for our four-legged friends. He's rarely offended by words and opinions, but admits to being very annoyed by animal cruelty. Refreshingly, he puts his money where his mouth is. I remember him once taking in two cats that he didn't really want. The owner had called him to ask if he wanted them, adding that he would drown them if Bernie refused. Of course, he said yes. One of the cats, Catty, recently turned 20.

I followed my friend towards a large hospitality suite called the Legends' Lounge. It was where he would be "warming up" guests before the match, as he often does. Along the way we passed several framed photographs of different Boro teams on the walls. Bernie was in there, but we barely glanced at any of them. I'd already seen many far more interesting photos of him, including one taken in 1990 with his Ireland teammates, manager Jack Charlton and the Pope during the World Cup in Italy.

Bernie, a Scot and a devout Catholic, was eligible for the Irish squad because of an Irish grandfather. I used to joke that he would have qualified to play for Ireland anyway, because he had an Irish Setter dog. As we entered the hospitality suite I heard several people engaged in the most important topic of the day: the upcoming match. At the time we were still pushing for promotion to the Premiership. Bernie immediately plunged into the discussion, and I tried my best to follow what he was saying. It seemed interesting, but I was having trouble understanding everything. Bernie has a strong Glaswegian accent and tends to speak quickly. If I get three-quarters of what he's saying, I think I'm doing well.

The Legends' Lounge is not just a crucible of conversation, it also serves food, and I was looking forward to a roast beef and Yorkshire pudding dinner with all the trimmings. I was starving as I'd deliberately missed lunch, expecting to eat at the ground. Bernie wouldn't join me for the meat, though; he's been a vegetarian for a few years now, and is well on the road to being vegan, for animal welfare, health and environmental reasons. "You write Middlesbrough off at your peril," he said, as we sat down before a waiter took our order for starters and drinks. Water for both of us; I was driving and Bernie is teetotal. "Still, I don't think we are going to win today," my friend continued, contradicting himself. "In three games, we've not won. Norwich have scored nearly double the number of goals we have, and they're 20 points ahead. You come here to get rid of your frustration and go home more frustrated."

To move away from the depressing turn in the conversation, I asked Bernie if he remembered the game we'd played together with Mark Proctor, another former Middlesbrough player. At the time Bernie still lived near me. He had a big garden and so decided it would be a good idea to lay out a small football pitch, so he could have the occasional kickabout. Bernie had installed full-size goals made by a Middlesbrough firm and also managed to acquire some nets from the old stadium at Ayresome Park. He had even bought some sawdust to mark out the pitch. It all came in very handy for a unique match that was arranged during an encounter at a Chinese takeaway in Middlesbrough. A worker there had recognised Bernie

Middlesbrough legends
George Hardwick
(bottom row, third from
left) and Wilf Mannion
(bottom row, fourth from
left) line up with the
England team,
circa 1948.

and asked if he fancied a game of football. Bernie agreed and got the takeaway guy to form a team. He then asked me and a few other friends to play for his side. I was over the moon at the thought of playing with both Bernie and Mark.

We also had Ali Brownlee, Bernie's fellow broadcaster, and a couple of lads who worked behind the scenes on their radio programme. Between us we were at least 200 years old; the Chinese team probably didn't think we looked like much of a foe. But it's a mistake to underestimate the skills retained by former professionals like Bernie. In his prime, he'd been a classic poacher who would much rather shoot than pass. He'd regularly turned tiny chances into goals. Mark had also been a very talented midfielder in his day, and their class shone through from the first kick. In contrast, I seem to recall tripping over my own feet or the grass a few times as I haphazardly passed the ball, trying not to look like the amateur I was.

In his own way, Bernie encouraged me every step of the way, regularly shouting: "Give me the ball!" as he hung around the goal waiting before doing what he did best: scoring over and over again, although the net wasn't really up to scratch, full of holes gnawed by cheeky rabbits. My friend pumped the air with his fist when he chalked up another goal, just as he'd always done in a "real" game. He didn't celebrate by jumping on the fence as he had so often done at Ayresome Park, though. He'd actually brought home some of that old fence and put it in his garden, though by the time I met him he'd already cut it up and framed it with a photo, then sold it. And anyway, he had a bit of a dodgy back; his jumping days were over. Overall, the Chinese takeaway guys barely touched the ball, and were thrashed soundly. But they took it on the chin and we made it up to them with a BBQ, even if their own sweet and sour chicken and fried rice were far tastier than the overcooked burgers and sausages grilled by Bernie's mate Colin. I felt ten feet tall after the match when Bernie told me: "You're just like Gareth Southgate!"

Returning the conversation to the present day, I said: "Middlesbrough are a bit boring to watch nowadays because they play such a negative style of football. They don't attack." Bernie agreed. "They are geared up solely to defend; to let the minimum number of goals in and try to win a game one-nil. I've been coming here for more than 30 years and we've played some crap games. The team have been rubbish and booed off before, but I have never heard so many boos as now. It's an indication of the brand of football they play." He was well and truly on a roll now. "There used to be more of a local connection. We would kiss the badge as they do now, but the majority of the lads back then were local lads, from Stockton, Middlesbrough and Redcar, devoted to their club. I was classed as a foreigner," he said. "And you were a bit older too," I pointed out. "The hairs used to stand up on the back of my neck to watch you work together and fight for one another. I always believed the team would pull something out of the bag. Now there are so many players on big contracts who know they won't be here next year. That's the sad reality." Then, with gloomy relish, I added: "Here one season, gone the next."

It was a relief to get some of the pessimism and negativity off my chest with someone who I knew felt the same way. Bernie and I are usually in tune, but even when we disagree I feel relaxed in his company. Our many discussions about football often remind me of times I spent chuntering with Alf and Jim. If we weren't talking about work, we'd more often than not be talking about football.

On Mondays, if we had a lull at work, we'd chat about the weekend's results, propped up against our ineffectual heater with steaming mugs of tea. Sometimes I'd regale them with stories of my own prowess in my local team or, more often, my disasters on the pitch. Donald would rather talk about fox hunting or pigeon racing, but the Wights – Alf and his son, Jim – were obsessed with football. I travelled with them many times to watch their team, Sunderland, even though my own football heart lay elsewhere, a few miles down the road to be precise. Alf was always a quiet man and he rarely swore. But the more I got to know him, the more I realised he would churn up inside when he watched a game.

My boss was so fond of football, his pen name was actually linked to the game; he chose "James Herriot" after seeing Scottish goal-keeper Jim Herriot on the television one day. And he often had two season tickets, alternating between Sunderland, where he was born, and Middlesbrough, closer to Thirsk so easier to get to. But it was Sunderland that was Alf's life-long obsession, despite growing up in Glasgow. His father's Sunderland fanaticism was contagious, and that's obviously who he got it from.

There's a lovely tale about Alf on a 1973 trip to Wembley, where he saw his team unexpectedly win the FA Cup final against big-shots Leeds United. After the match, he found himself dancing for joy with a stranger, a smart gentleman in a camel coat. Alf was so thrilled by the result of the match he felt that from then on, he could die happy. He was very proud when he became Life President of Sunderland Football Club a few years before his death. But, typically, he didn't accept the free seats he was offered in the directors' box; he chose to watch from the stands, just as he'd always done.

Back in the Boro stadium, Bernie and I were by now talking to a couple of his fans sitting at our table. Paul Arkley, who'd brought his teenage daughter Georgia to the match, reminded me, because of his short and sharp haircut, of the Terminator, played by Arnold Schwarzenegger (although Paul has a northern accent, not an Austrian one). Not unexpectedly, people like to talk to me about animals and as we all tucked into our pre-match meal, Paul said he often helped to muck out on the farm where his girlfriend rides horses. One horse had stood on his finger and he'd had to go to hospital. But it wasn't our chat about the animal kingdom that was the most interesting topic: it was Paul's adoration of Bernie that captured my imagination.

About four years ago, before the two of them had ever met, Paul decided to have a permanent tribute to the retired footballer inked onto his body. He told me he has other tattoos but, wearing a smart white polo shirt when we met in the Legends' Lounge, the only one fully on display was a running and serious-looking Bernie in his football kit. Yes, incredible as it might seem, Paul has a tattoo of Bernie on his left arm. It runs from wrist to elbow and also includes a favourite Boro chant: "You are my Boro, my only Boro, you make me happy when skies are grey." Paul explained why he'd felt compelled to get the tattoo. Not for the first time did I hear the words: "Bernie's a legend in my lifetime." Paul said Bernie had been the most prolific goalscorer in his time as a Middlesbrough supporter. For him, it was as simple as that.

Remember Paul had gone ahead with the tribute on his skin before he'd actually met Bernie. But fate was to play its part. Paul recalled that the day after his arm had been so expertly punctured and painted – "by a man with no passion for football" – he had, almost unbelievably, stumbled across his hero in real life. He'd gone with his girlfriend and her son to watch the lad play football, on a pitch that just happened to be near to where Bernie, unbeknown to them, was coaching some other youngsters. Paul's girlfriend was the first to spot Bernie. She turned to her boyfriend and said, with a touch of comic understatement: "I've just seen that chap who's on your arm. He's over there." The tattooist must surely have been at the top of his game if the flesh-and-blood footballer could be recognised from a picture on a forearm. Paul and Bernie have met several times since then. Bernie is both flattered and bemused by his likeness on Paul's skin. "I love Morrissey, but I wouldn't get a tattoo of him," my friend said, before adding: "A guy I met in Debenhams has one of me on his shin."

Back at the hospitality suite we finished admiring Paul's tattoo as I wolfed down my last couple of mouthfuls of roast beef and Yorkshire pudding. I had a brief appointment before the game and, right on time, a teenage lad appeared to usher me through a door and into the stands, which were still filling up. I followed him up and down several different flights of steps as we discussed Bernie tattoos, before he told me that he'd once seen Bernie dressed up as Santa Claus. We finally arrived at a small room high up in the stadium, with a great view of the pitch through a huge window. I was there to be filmed with several others for a video that was being made about Bernie's career, called *Slaven Strikes 100*. The man who interviewed me was initially distracted because he'd lost his car keys but, a true professional, he got on with the job and we spent a pleasant few minutes discussing choice moments of my friend's footballing life.

"So many iconic times," I said. "When Bernie scored he'd leap on the fence or wall and his adoring public would reach out to try to touch him." It happened a lot, I remembered, and it was fun to see, even if occasionally he almost came a cropper. He'd once jumped on a fence after scoring during a big game against Newcastle and a little boy, hoisted up on someone's shoulders, began excitedly pulling on Bernie's shirt, unintentionally pulling my friend towards a big drop. Luckily, he didn't fall, and the experience didn't stop Bernie's extravagant celebrations. He didn't always get everything right, though. Bernie was well known for his extremely annoying habit of often finding himself offside. "I'd be watching the fella with the flag to see if it would go up and there'd be groans around me as it did. Then cries of, 'Slaven, not again'," I told the interviewer.

Being forced to cast my mind back for the video made me think about events I'd not thought about in years, such as a frightening away match I went to against Chelsea in 1988. Middlesbrough was flying high back then in the Second Division. We were battling for the final promotion place with Chelsea. The winner of the two-legged final would be promoted to what was then known as the First Division. We'd won 2-0 at home; this was the return leg. I'd made sure I wasn't on call for work so I could go down to London to watch the game with friends. We didn't think Chelsea supporters would lay out the red carpet for us, but neither did we expect the welcome we did receive. On the King's Road our bus was pelted with bottles and bricks. There were no police to be seen. (They were later soundly criticised for not being up to scratch that day.) Dodging flying debris and feeling very vulnerable, we ran to Stamford Bridge, Chelsea's home ground. Only once we were inside did I notice that my legs were shaking. When I calmed down I began wondering if we'd make it out alive after the match.

I was right to be worried. We lost the match 1-0 but won on aggregate, which meant we were promoted and Chelsea were relegated. Their fans did not react well. The Battle of Stamford Bridge took place in 1066 in Yorkshire, but when the final whistle blew there was another more modern version. Some Chelsea fans began invading the pitch, unable to control their frustration and anger. Bernie (who'd scored in the first leg) hadn't a clue what was going on. He hurtled towards the Boro supporters to celebrate, just as he always did. I stood open-mouthed, watching Chelsea fans behind him on the grass, police officers on horseback among them. Sir Stuart Bell, Middlesbrough MP at the time, was at the match and later described the fans running amok as "like the hordes of Genghis Khan". As the melee continued behind Bernie, he carried on running towards us, his adoring fans. He was still enjoying the occasion, but then he suddenly looked over his shoulder. Clearly shocked to see the fracas, he immediately swerved and shot down the tunnel; he always had been able to react quickly, but I'd never seen him sprint like that. At least one fan and a police officer were injured that day, but I'm glad to say Bernie – and everyone else – made it to safety.

Three decades later, safe and sound and back in the Legends' Lounge, there wasn't much time left before kick-off. Bernie suddenly stood up and beckoned me to follow him. We crossed the room and I found myself standing near the much-depleted carvery, gazing around at several tables of excitable Boro fans. It was time for Bernie to say a few words. Microphone in hand, he wondered aloud how the team would do that day, before introducing me and asking a few questions, like why I loved football more than cricket. "I was crap at cricket at school," I said. Ever the wag, he enjoyed telling the crowd

I'd taken Lin on our first date to an abattoir. "No! We went to the knacker's yard," I corrected him. "A cow needed a post-mortem. I couldn't cancel it, so Lin came with me."

A few minutes later, I was almost beside myself with excitement because I was going to do something that few fans have had the privilege of doing: walking out onto the pitch. I moved briskly through a labyrinth of stairs and corridors before entering and exiting the tunnel to, finally, arrive on that hallowed playing surface. It was my first opportunity to stand where I'd seen my team win and lose so many times before. The players hadn't yet appeared, but the noise from the stands was still deafening. Later, I'd learn there were almost 24,000 people there that day. Almost immediately, and a little surprisingly, I saw one of Skeldale's clients among the crowd. It's amazing who you bump into. I went over to say hello, chuckling to myself as I passed a sporty-looking man in a tracksuit vigorously chewing his gum. Ability to chew like there's no tomorrow must be written in his job description, I thought.

I was briefly, and pleasantly, distracted from my nervousness about the game to come by four local siblings and their friend, who'd formed a band called Cattle and Cane. They stood a few feet from me performing their popular ode to Middlesbrough called *Infant Hercules*. Its lyrics, printed on the inside collar of the Boro's shirts, tell the story of the area's industrial rise and fall. The song's title is inspired by the words of the 19th-century prime minister and statesman, William Gladstone, who visited Middlesbrough in 1862 when it was becoming an industrial powerhouse. "This remarkable place, the youngest child of England's enterprise, is an infant, but if an infant, an infant Hercules," he said. Sadly, Middlesbrough is not as strong as it was in Gladstone's day, but

Cattle and Cane's haunting song deftly captures the hope for Middlesbrough's future. My own heart swelled as the youngsters sang and played their hearts out. "Men built from steel, women just as strong… A small town with bigger hearts and voices to be heard… The world won't forget Infant Hercules."

Would the match to come be one that was best forgotten? Norwich were a good team, so I had my doubts about the result. I looked up, not for inspiration from above, but to see if I could spot the club's owner, Steve Gibson OBE, in his seat. The Middlesbrough-born, self-made millionaire had been a vital player in the consortium that saved the club from liquidation in 1986. He later bankrolled the Boro and we went on to win our first ever trophy in 2004, the League Cup. We even reached the 2006 UEFA Cup Final. But that was then, and this was now. I couldn't see Steve but was sure he would be watching, although I knew he didn't have a magic wand to return us to our heyday. None of us did.

As my mind wandered, the two teams suddenly appeared and the stadium erupted. I managed to take some photos before I was quickly shown to my seat in the stands next to Bernie; I'd never have found it, or him, left to my own devices. The game was finally on. As it turned out, it wasn't the most exciting of matches. We had a hatful of chances to score, but couldn't put it in the back of the net. It was all very frustrating, as football too often is. At times I was more interested in what was going on in the stands. I was sitting with men I considered to be football royalty. As well as Bernie, there was John Hendrie, another former Middlesbrough player revered by fans, and a retired referee called Jeff Winter. While I did call out occasionally to spur on my team and joined in a brief chant, I felt anxious more than anything, not helped by the unfriendly and unwelcome booing I occasionally heard. At half time it was still 0-0 and I consoled myself with the fact that at least we weren't behind, while Bernie made notes for his after-match commentary and Jeff, a local man, shared his thoughts. His take on things was interesting. "As a former referee, I agree with referees more than the fans do," he said. An obvious point, perhaps, but I hadn't really thought about it before. Jeff grew up with Gazza (former Newcastle and England player Paul Gascoigne), "one of my all-time favourite players," he said. The referee had once officiated at an FA Cup final; I was more than a little impressed.

Any football fan would enjoy chatting to Jeff for hours, but there was another half to watch. I leaned over to Bernie and told him I thought the Boro's chances of promotion were fading fast. "If we get promotion this year, I'll go full frontal!" he said, adding: "I can assure you, you're safe." I knew exactly what he was referring to and burst out laughing. He was talking about a hilarious incident just before Christmas in 1998, when he was still a match commentator. That season Middlesbrough was in the Premiership. When asked about the team's chances at a forthcoming fixture away to Manchester United, Bernie had said on live radio that their chances were slim. Well, he didn't quite put it like that. What he actually said was that if Middlesbrough won he would bare his backside in the window of Binns, a well-known Middlesbrough department store. Bernie didn't for a second think he would have to do a "moonie". After all, Boro hadn't beaten Manchester United for almost 70 years.

Football is full of surprises. Middlesbrough defender Gary Pallister joked afterwards that it was Bernie's dare that had spurred Middlesbrough on that day: "It was all the motivation we needed," he said. Whether the thought of my friend's naked bottom really did have something to do with the result, no one knows, but the Boro turned in a fantastic performance. We beat all the odds by winning 3-2 at Old Trafford. It was a result greeted with great joy by the travelling Boro fans, who immediately started chanting: "Bernie, Bernie, show us your arse!" much to the bemusement of those who hadn't heard the rash promise made the week before.

Bernie is not a man to break his word, so on the Monday after the match he turned up at the manager's office at Binns. There, he put on his red tartan kilt and made his way slowly through the shop to its front. "As I entered the store window I couldn't believe my eyes," he said. "There were a couple of thousand people out front all hoping to get a glimpse of my backside. If only I had kept my big mouth shut." Bernie turned around, bent over and whipped up his kilt – to reveal the numbers "three" and "two" that had been written on his buttocks by a brave volunteer.

Turning my eyes and thoughts to the game again, it wasn't long before Onel Hernandez's beautiful strike ensured victory for Norwich. They won 1-0. It was our fourth defeat in a row. "Well, that's that," I said to myself. Bernie and I smiled bravely as we posed for a few photographs with fans. But I had little time to stand around analysing and fretting; I needed to get away, because I was back on call later that evening. My friend and I said our goodbyes and I made my way through throngs of disappointed football fans. One of them stopped me near a flight of stairs and asked for my autograph for his wife, Rosalind. I rummaged around in my jacket pocket for a *Yorkshire Vet* photo, and signed it. Scrawling my name and chatting about the TV programme for a couple of minutes made me forget, just for a moment, all about my football woes. But before long the fan had wandered away clutching his signed memento and, once again, my mind turned to the disheartening game I'd just witnessed. There is, of course, a life outside football and other things that are important, but right at that moment, it just didn't feel like that was true. As the late, great Liverpool manager Bill Shankly once said: "Some people think football is a matter of life and death. I can assure you, it's much more serious than that."

Me (top row, second from right) at Sessay Primary School aged 9.

Back at the beginning

'd been to some of the best bits of Yorkshire, but I thought I'd finish at the beginning, so to speak. That's how I found myself standing in my Granny Wright's dark kitchen, leaning against the sink near the only window, enjoying a wide-ranging discussion on trees, dogs, and rugs.

I was chatting to Graham Hodgson, the man who now lives in my granny's house. He told me his grandmother had made rugs with bits of old material, just as my own granny had done. Both had been handy and hardworking ladies, I thought to myself. Graham was a Skeldale client, often bringing in his two dogs and I was in his kitchen, in the village of Thirkleby, not far from Thirsk, because Graham had kindly invited me in for a peek.

It was a few minutes before I realised with amazement that I'd last stood in that underlit room half a century ago, when I was a scrawny 13-year-old.

I find myself looking back on life on a fairly regular basis these days. I wouldn't want to actually go back in time; the past is the past and what's done is done. But reviewing and accepting what's gone before can help us to make the most of the here and now. It is, I think, a natural process as we age. At any rate, travelling back to the start is surely one way to prepare for a more contented ending. Although I was feeling sentimental, standing in the heart of my granny's former home near a small sign saying: "Keep smiling, the best is yet to come", I was enjoying being there and enjoying my conversation with Graham.

I'm only a decade older than him and we'd just discovered our childhoods in North Yorkshire were very similar. He's a mechanic, but we both grew up on farms, just 11 miles apart. We both enjoyed playing in fields, streams and woods. We also had to do chores: feeding calves, collecting eggs, sorting potatoes and chopping wood. We'd been surrounded by animals, from cows, pigs and sheep to geese, chickens and ferrets. Suddenly, Graham wrenched me back to the present, telling me that his three-year-old black Pointer, Blade, had lost a litter of puppies two weeks before her due date. I sympathised and automatically began doling out veterinary advice, something I'd never done before in my granny's kitchen.

Granny Wright's two-bedroomed cottage, which belonged to the nearby Manor Farm, was as familiar to me as my own home next door, where I was born and lived with my parents and younger brother. The pair of us shared a double bed until we moved house in 1970. We left because my father, a farm labourer and the son of Manor Farm's manager, found a new job in a village a few miles away. Now here I was back in Thirkleby, lingering for a while to soak up its timeless ambience. Naturally some things had altered. "Our kitchen table was where the bed for your dog is now," I said. "And where your worktop is, there was an armchair, where my granny's brother liked to stretch out." I opened Graham's pantry door and peered in, noticing the old stone shelves were gone. "It was lovely and cool in here, we didn't have a fridge," I said. "There was usually a cut of cold meat, covered over with mesh to keep the flies off. And we kept a jug of fresh milk here as well, with a couple of inches of cream on the top." Graham smiled; he too had drunk the same fresh, delicious milk growing up.

I noticed the kitchen had no fireplace; I remembered there had been one back in my day. "The house was mostly damp and cold, though," I recalled. "It still is," said Graham. Then, standing under the wooden-beamed ceiling in his small front room, which the Wrights had only used for special occasions, we laughed when I said my grandad had once chopped up some old Windsor chairs for firewood. "They'd have been antiques now," Graham pointed out, as I noticed a framed drawing of his dog Blade hanging on the wall where a grandfather clock had once stood. I was glad the clock had eventually made its way to my brother David's home, while a lovingly polished old desk, in our family for six generations, had come to me. It has taken pride of place in my own living room for years.

In Graham's back garden I said hello to his gorgeous Rottweiler, Busser, clearly used to being bossed around by the enthusiastic and charming Blade. I suddenly experienced a flashback. Fifty-odd years beforehand, Pip, a collie dog at the farm, had bitten me on the cheek while I sat stroking her. She drew blood, but didn't do any lasting damage. I absentmindedly touched my face, the scene of Pip's "crime", as I wandered around out back on old cobbles and new concrete, looking at all the wildflowers Graham had planted and the butterflies and bees flying around. "Bumblebees have taken over a bird's nest in one of the outbuildings," he said. I didn't see the nest, but I did see chopped wood stacked up in the very same place my grandparents had kept theirs, and felt a wave of nostalgia. "It's just wood," I reminded myself. I gazed at the washhouse where my granny had toiled for hours on end to get her sheets and table-cloths whiter than white. In another small building I remembered chunks of meat hanging from ceiling hooks after my grandad had slaughtered a pig. He was a versatile chap, even acting as the village barber sometimes; I still have his old clippers.

But not everything at Graham's was attached to a fond memory. I recalled with distaste the outdoor toilet we'd used, even in the winter, and the man who arrived regularly to collect the waste. My grandparents eventually had an indoor loo built, just as everyone else did. I never found out what the man did for work after that.

Climbing over a fence into the field next door, I stood by a couple of trees, pleased they were still there. They were two of many I'd plucked apples from as a child. "I take two apples to work each day, they are super sweet," Graham said with obvious pleasure. "They glow red in the sun." We reminisced for a bit about heavenly family vegetable plots (he refuses to eat supermarket carrots because they don't taste of much), before I picked out the spot where my family's hen houses had stood. I remembered a fire that had killed all the chicks one year, and a fox that had slaughtered the hens in another.

My mind, then, briefly stayed focused on scary memories; I felt worried all over again as I recalled accidentally pushing a garden fork through my brother's foot in the 1960s. It could have been far nastier than it was. Luckily, the antibiotics worked. As I left Graham and walked down towards Manor Farm itself, a few cows watched as I passed a horse chestnut tree. My friends and I would often scale its branches before the conkers were ready. Decades later, I could almost hear our laughter.

I would have liked to have knocked on the door of the farmhouse kitchen and have a cup of tea with the farmer, Jonathan Trenholme, but I'd heard he was on holiday for his wife's 50th birthday. I knew, though, that he wouldn't mind me having a quiet nose around in the playground of my childhood. I walked past the rambling old house, thinking about Jonathan and some of its other occupants, including tenant farmer, Norman Knowles. He'd lived there when I was in Thirkleby, although Jonathan's grandmother had owned the place. Jonathan himself moved to the village as a child in 1972, after I'd left. When Mr Knowles retired from farming Jonathan was only 21, but nevertheless he decided to take the farm on. He's been there ever since, and nowadays has about 60 suckler cows and 300 acres of land. He grows wheat, barley, beans and oats and, although it might all sound good, it hasn't been easy. Jonathan's had no choice but to ring the many changes. Like all farmers, he's had to deal with increased mechanisation, more regulations and higher costs. He can't afford many staff, he says, and the days when my old bosses, Alf and Donald, had time to visit lots of small farms like his seem an awfully long time ago. "When I first started out I was given three sheep," Jonathan told me not long ago. "There was a lambing problem and Donald turned up to sort it out. He would have been in his 70s."

I walked on through the farmyard, noticing the little church off in the distance where several of my ancestors were buried, and a wood where I used to play with my mates. We'd made dens in there and acted out cops and robbers. I remembered that, before I was born, a Second World War bomber had crashed in another wood a few miles away, when Jonathan's mother Cathy was a teenager. Five men had died. Cathy had walked to the crash site and was shocked to see thousands of dead birds, something she never forgot. "It was a carpet of birds, right there in the woods," she would often say. "Poor them – and those poor men."

It was a sobering thought and, as I meandered around the farm-yard, I tried not to be too miserable about the passing of time. But that's sometimes easier said than done. As I stood in the remains of what was a cow house in Mr Knowles' time, I couldn't help visualising the cows coming in; each of them walking to the exact same spot twice daily. A smaller building, where calves had been kept in the 1950s and 60s, was empty, other than rubbish, and I spotted a couple of dead rats on the floor. There was no longer any corn in the granary, although the steps my father and his workmates would slowly walk up with 100 kg, full-to-the-brim hessian sacks on their backs were still there. I climbed them, also slowly, empty-handed and with a heavy heart.

To try to cheer myself up, I walked down into the village. My parents, grandparents and many other characters from my youth are now six feet under, but a handful are still around, including horse breeders the Ramsays. Unfortunately for me, the couple had moved away, only a few days before my visit. I'd just missed them. I was disappointed as I walked past their old home, then heartened to see Bill Ludiman, a longstanding Skeldale client, smiling as he peered at me from a second-floor window in the house he's lived in for 45 years. He moved in not long after the death of its former owner George Barker, who was known as Thirkleby's resident miser when I was a boy. It turned out George wasn't so miserly after all, leaving all his money to a local family and to a children's charity. Bill, a widower in his 80s, called out to me from what I still think of as George's old cottage, shirtless on a boiling hot day and preparing to go out and sit in his garden.

It was almost time to leave, but not before I'd driven past my other granny's old home. I wanted to see the old clock on her outside wall.

It hadn't worked when I was a child, although I'd often fiddled with the mechanism, which was accessed through a bedroom, and then rushed downstairs and outside to see if the hands had moved. They hadn't. The clock still didn't work and, for some reason, I was glad about it. I was also happy to see my grandparents' garden was still overflowing with flowers. I stopped for a few minutes at the village hall and saw a green defibrillator as well as adverts for Pilates and a daily delivery of newspapers.

Then I sat on a bench dedicated to Frederick Cyril Sherwood, 1919-2005, "from his many friends in the village." Good old Cyril, I thought (for that was what we all called him). During the war he'd worked in the signal box in a village up the road and played football against Italian prisoners. Later he'd run the post office and village shop (it sold mouth-watering gobstoppers) with his wife Ruth, the blacksmith's daughter. Cyril also trained with a local running group well into his old age. As a child I'd known his father-in-law, Bill Armstrong, who I've mentioned before. He was so skilled at his job he'd once sold a re-shoed horse back to the expert Newcastle dealer he'd bought it from a few days before, for a tidy profit. The man had thought the animal he'd sold to Bill was lame and didn't realise he'd purchased the very same horse until he got her home.

I left such thoughts and the village behind and drove a mile or so up the road for my last stop of the day, an old prisoner-of-war camp for Italians, made up of several derelict huts, lots of weeds and a huge water tower that had awed me as a child. The prisoners were gone by the time I was born but I knew security must have been pretty lax in Yorkshire's wartime countryside; my parents had gone to a few dances with some detainees. My father enjoyed propping up the bar; he was far better known for his banter than his moves on the dance floor. But I like to imagine my mother forgetting all about her many chores and laughing while being twirled around by Giuseppe, Giovanni and Roberto. As a child Chris Greensit, the farmer who found the hoard of Civil War coins, met prisoners on his family's farm, who'd come to pick potatoes. Alf also mentioned them, including an Italian man who helped him catch a big bullock by grabbing its ear. Another time, four German prisoners used their considerable strength to pull down hard on a rope, working with Alf to get a cow's dislocated hipbone back in its socket. He used that story in one of his books.

'Danke schon!' I said fervently, and I really meant it. 'Bitte! Bitte!' they cried, all smiles. They had enjoyed the whole thing and I had the feeling that this would be one of the tales they would tell when they returned to their homes.

It was now time for me to go home, where the garden was waiting for my attention. I was looking forward to spending a few hours with Lin, just pottering around. When I walked in, she handed me a cup of tea and we wandered out into the back. It was a bright summer's evening and the flowers and vegetables looked lovely, as they always do at this time of year. I could see the green fields of Yorkshire all around, as far the eye could see. "It's not a bad life," I said to no one in particular, as I bent down and began digging up some new potatoes for our tea.

ACKNOWLEDGEMENTS

Many thanks to Peter and Lin for their time, chats and hospitality. A lot of other people gave up their time too, from brief emails and phone calls to long chats/tours with cuppas and biscuits. Thanks to all of them, in no particular order: Thirsk librarians, the Greens, Philip and Janet Shaw, Bryan and Vicky Smart, the North Yorkshire Moors Railway (particularly Kieran Murray), Raymond, Andrew and Wendy Hunter, Thirsk Market stallholders, Lee and Maisie in York. Chris Greensit, Yorkshire Museum's Andrew Woods, Stephen Wombwell and volunteers at Newburgh Priory, Bernie Slaven, The Wheatsheaf Inn, Caroline Howard and Askham Bryan Wildlife and Conservation Park. The Hornshaws, Emma Dawber, Thirsk Museum's Jim Seymour and other volunteers, Thirsk volunteer tourguides Ted Naisbitt and John Fisher. Zarina Belk, Tom Banks, Ryedale Folk Museum, Jane and Toby Whittaker, Josephine Runciman and Graham Evison at Yorkshire Gliding Club, Andrew Routh, Graham Hodgson, Jonathan Trenholme, Sarah Beckerlegge, Ian Ashton, York Minster and Street Paws' Fiona Willis. Finally, last, but never least, thanks to Micky for having my back, again.

Helen Leavey has been a journalist for 20 years and worked for the BBC in London and Taiwan. She lived for a decade in China, where she tried her best to multi-task, as mum, journalist and Mandarin student, as well as holding down a job in human rights. Her love of the environment came into sharp focus in Beijing, where clean air, trees and grass were all too rare. Helen is a southerner, born and brought up in Slough, long before its already unsavoury reputation nose-dived with *The Office*. She now enjoys life in the North with her husband, a Yorkshireman who's been able to explain some of his county's more unusual words and traditions. They have two children.